And I'd Do It Again

AIMÉE CROCKER was an American heiress,
Bohemian, world traveler and author best
known for her adventures in the Far East,
her extravagant parties and her collections
of husbands and lovers, adopted children,
Buddhas, tattoos and snakes.

Aimée Crocker

And I'd Do It Again

HEAD
ZEUS

Published in the UK in 2017 by Head of Zeus, Ltd
This paperback edition published in 2017 by Head of Zeus, Ltd

9 7 5 3 2 4 6 8

A catalogue record for this book is available
from the British Library.

ISBN (PB): 9781784979867
ISBN (E): 9781784979843

Typeset by Adrian McLaughlin

Printed and bound in Great Britain by
CPI Group (UK) Ltd, Croydon CR0 4YY

Head of Zeus Ltd
First Floor East
5–8 Hardwick Street
London ECIR 4RG

WWW.HEADOFZEUS.COM

FOREWORD
BY HELEN LEDERER

A s a child, I had a best friend whose parents encouraged her to paint murals on their kitchen wall. Oddly, when I tried this at home, my Bohemian artwork (biro on wallpaper) was not met with the same enthusiasm. But I always wanted to be different; I was always attracted to the unconventional ways of having fun.

I mention this because Aimée Crocker's memoirs will appeal to the lurking adventuress in us all. From an early age, Aimée knew she would reject her conventional upbringing to travel and discover other cultures. And while her 'calling' was possibly more noble than my yen to become a small, fat show-off (as one school report would have it), we both share a spirit of curiosity and a distinct unease with convention; Aimée's abhorrence of the mundane oozes from almost every page of this beguiling book.

Born into affluence, Aimée was the daughter of a judge whose family was well-heeled and well-known. She was sent to a finishing school in Europe and then, presumably, was expected to find a suitable aristocrat to marry.

But Aimée had other ideas. Instead of returning home, she set sail for the Far East almost immediately. She canoed down crocodile infested rivers, was seduced by men of dubious pedigree, and on one occasion had a brush with a snake prompting a rather unusual erotic awakening. But thankfully, Aimée embraced these discoveries without apology or compromise. Her need for wit from her fellows, her cheerful enthusiasm for the male body and her deep fascination with other ways of life, made her a woman of hope and adventure. She was as honest as she was naïve and in my view, it's better to be naïve and give yourself up to experience, than to stay home and miss the party.

Aimée was a trailblazer and her book is a characterful reminder of how far we have come, particularly if you incline towards authenticity and a freedom of spirit over the limitations of stereotypes. At a time when women were expected to take an interest in fabrics and wifely duties in the home, Aimée was gamely traversing continents, behaving as little like a tourist as possible.

She threw herself at new worlds with humility, openness and 'pushiness' and despite a near fatal train accident, a beheading from a Bornean head hunter, a narrow escape from a rampant warlord and losing to Oscar Wilde in a drinking game, Aimée triumphed.

A true original, her steely determination to bypass social strictures and have a 'lark', made for a colourful if eventful life. Such antics would not have been considered suitable behaviour at the time for her contemporaries, but Aimée broke rules. She followed her impulses and passions, flouting convention whenever she could.

Today we celebrate 21st century pioneers such as Cheryl Strayed who hiked the Pacific Crest Trail solo and Junko Tabei, the first woman to climb Mount Everest. We no longer dismiss such women as 'eccentric'. We admire their strength and bravery. But let us also include Aimée Crocker in this canvas of women who followed their dreams. Admittedly her adventures are marginally less athletic, but her pleasure in the telling of them calls out to the Bohemian in all of us.

And if the abundance of death and drama makes some of you wonder if it could all be true, I would encourage the doubting Thomasinas among you to go with the spirit of adventure. It is always better to travel than to arrive. And have fun. Bon voyage.

PREFACE

This book is not to be mistaken for an apology. Not at all.

If I have lived fully and richly I thank God for it. My only regrets are for the things that I have not done and for the experiences I have not had. Also for the people I have not known.

I believe absolutely that living, in the completest sense of that word . . . discovering the full beauty of living and plunging one's self utterly into the human beings that swarm through this life . . . is a pure art. It is, I honestly think, the highest artistic accomplishment we can hope for. All the recognized arts . . . your paintings, your sculpture, your music, your books . . . all those things are only the symbols of that higher art: living.

I have been accused of living adventurously. Let us admit the word. But I have never been an "adventuress." If I have never cared about your man-made conventions (and every modern schoolgirl would laugh at those of my day), I was not immoral, but un-moral. If I have often loved, I have at least loved well and fully. I have nothing to be ashamed of, in spite of the scandalous press reports that hopeful reporters managed to use to amuse a scandal-loving public. And if I have dared to stick my nose into trouble just because the game was fun, does it make me a brazen hussy?

No, this is not an apology.

It is the recollections of a woman who is no longer young and who has crowded a great deal of movement and fun and action

and love and adventure into a lifetime now drawing towards
its close.

And if I could live it again, this very long life of mine,
I would love to do so. And the only difference would be that I
would try to crowd in still more ... more places, more things,
more women, more men, more love, more excitement.

Let the Mrs. Grundys arch their eyebrows and reach for their
smelling salts.

CHAPTER I

Charles Crocker, uncle of Aimée, was the founder of the Central Pacific Railroad. Portrait *c.* 1972 by Stephen W. Shaw.

It does not matter in the least about my early childhood except for three things. I choose these because they had a bearing on the rest of my life.

I was born a Crocker of San Francisco, which is another way of saying that I had the "golden spoon" in my mouth. The Crocker family needs no introduction nor comment. For those who never read the papers I might say that we were exceedingly wealthy.

Infancy and childhood passed in the Californian metropolis. I was very much like any other child. I had the same fun, same naughtinesses, same prodigiousnesses. Why bore you with all that? Those three things of my young girlhood that matter are a vision I had and two childish passions.

The vision came to me first before I had reached my teens. It was in Sacramento, in a huge, roomy, comfortable house. I can still remember the details and the arrangement and the atmosphere but it does not matter. One moonlight night I ran ahead of my nurse upstairs, when it was time to go to bed. I was not afraid of the dark, I remember, but rather enjoyed it. I cannot say now whether I felt an exhilaration or any sort of an "odd" feeling, although it is possible that I did. When I think of that experience now it is so entwined in later experiences, so almost frightful, that I am not sure.

Whether or not, I ran ahead of Nurse and got to my room before she reached my stairs. The moonlight was pouring in the large bay window and shone directly on my bed. I could see very plainly, stretched out on my white bedspread, a woman.

I knew she was very beautiful but I could not see her features because they were covered over with a veil of some gossamer material up to her eyes, and she was dressed in colored silk robes, a costume such as I had never seen, even in pictures. There she lay, radiant and shining, her arms stretched back on the bed, and looking straight at me. She smiled, I remember. She seemed to know me.

And it was somehow ... I can hardly explain it ... as though I knew her, too; as though she were there naturally, as if she *belonged* to me.

I was not frightened, but I was excited. I ran back to the stairs and called out to Nurse who was lumbering up, and I told her to hurry. I remember that I did not say why. Good old Nurse ran up as fast as her heavy legs could carry her, thinking something had happened to me. But when she came into my room, and there was nothing wrong at all, she was angry. Actually the woman on the bed had disappeared as soon as I moved to call Nurse. The whole incident had taken about ten seconds.

I tried to tell Nurse about it, but it was no use. I knew perfectly well that I *had* seen some one on the bed, but to her simple, honest and awfully practical mind it was all stuff and nonsense.

But twenty years later I was to see this same vision again, clearly and unforgettably, and a very wise man was to explain to me what it meant, or rather just enough of what it meant to open up, just a crack of the way, the doorway through which the age-old wisdom of the East is able to look back along the curious streets of Life and to see what all our science and our Western "knowledge" has never even suspected.

And, perhaps if that very wise man had been able to tell me about it in those days when I was a child, I would have been able to understand it more fully. At all events I felt more fully, and I have always believed that children in their simplicity are a little closer to that great understanding which is so remarkable a part of the Orient.

And I shall see this vision once more before I die. That same very wise man told me so, and I believe it utterly. It will be the end, then. It frightens me. Not that I am afraid to die, but rather afraid of the great mystery of death, afraid of what I do not understand, of things that I have seen strange vague glimpses of during this curious life of mine.

So much for the vision. The two childish passions are more difficult to explain because there is no real story in them. Perhaps the best way is to say plainly that everything that smelled or reminded me of or in any way suggested the Orient had a fascination for me from the day of my vision.

Pearls, for instance. I adored them. I used to save all my allowance money for them. I had a miniature collection when I was very young. The more sparkling stones ... diamonds, emeralds, rubies ... they were all pretty pieces of glass to me. But pearls *said* something to me. I could not have told you what they said, but they were alive to me. And later on in life, when I was able to have some of the loveliest pearls, I discovered that I made them glow, gave them luster, just by wearing them or touching them. Women have often asked me to wear their pearls just to restore their lost luster.

When I was still in pigtails I could sit for hours with a beautiful pearl pendant of Mother's, watching the liquid color-changes, feeling them warm in my hand. I believe pearls hypnotized me in some strange way. Certainly they had some influence upon me, and to this day it has never ceased. It is all wrapped up in this power of the East over me, a power which has never dimmed, which has never left me, even though I am now too old to go there, to the world where my life blossomed. And if you could see the brown bodies of the pearl fishers going down, knife in teeth, to bring up the precious drops of iridescence for the trade, if you could see the clusters of them that stud the head-dress of some haughty, obese and sulky harem favorite, as I have seen them, you would understand how much of the soul of the Orient glows in the mysterious luster of pearls.

Very young indeed was I when the finger of the East reached out across the Pacific and touched me. For instance I had a Chinese bed which I picked out for myself when I was only ten years old. That was my other childish passion. It is not a very important incident, perhaps, nor a very entertaining story, but it is just one more key to my later life.

Ten years old, I was. Perhaps a trifle older. I was to be given a bed of my very own. My mother took me into the shopping district of San Francisco and we looked at a great many good old-fashioned, mid-Victorian beds. None of them interested me very much and I paid little attention to them. But while we were walking about we looked into some sort of an antique shop and there I saw a bed ... a bed of exquisitely carved teak-wood, canopied like a little house. I could feel that it was alive with something of me, I could feel that it was trying to speak to me. I had never seen nor heard of a Chinese bed, but I knew perfectly well that it was for me. It is the only way I can express what I felt. Children all will know what I mean.

So I set up a cry for the bed (I dare say it was ridiculously expensive) and nothing would quiet me until my mother had paid for it and ordered it sent home at once. I slept in my Chinese bed that very night and I have slept in one ever since, even to this day, whenever I have not been traveling. I have had others, but never one that was so close to something inexpressible in me as that first one.

As I say, this little incident does not seem very important and yet I know now that it showed something very definite about me, young as I was. My life was to prove it.

But let me go on with my story.

Up to the age of fourteen I was a little savage. My family moved about from San Francisco to Sacramento and back again. I was spoiled and indulged and let run wild and pampered. I played about the water fronts like a young beachcomber. I baby-flirted with the sailors and the sea-captains who all gave me little things from the other side of the world across the blue Pacific, and told me endless stories. Incidentally, I learned to swear then. I guess that was about all I learned, too, because my schooling was shamefully neglected until I was getting to be quite a big girl.

Then my parents decided that I should go to Europe and be educated. So off I was packed with a party of other California girls of wealthy parents under the chaperonage of Mrs. C. who turned out to be pretty much of a failure as the guardian of the young, prankish and romantic little imps that we were.

We went to Dresden. We went to one of those curious schools which Europe creates especially for American girls where you learn nothing at all of any practical value or educational merit, but where you learn to act like a duchess, to flirt outrageously, to wear the clothes of a society woman ten years older than your age, to smoke, to drink and to carry on with the handsome, heel-clicking young officers of the court in their musical comedy uniforms. And if the chaperon is the same sort as Mrs. C. you learn to do a number of things that would make dear old Victorian mothers reach for their prayer-books.

But all in all it was rather fun, and I seriously believe it gives poise, and that is what a woman needs more than anything else in life.

Mrs. C., as I have already suggested, was not a model duenna. Excellent woman, of good social standing in San Francisco, her fortune needed padding a little, and she had consequently "consented" to escort this little party of girls abroad for finishing. She was well-meaning and sweet, but the fact that her young charges were daughters of some of the wealthiest citizens of California was too much for her. She attempted to do things in the grand manner, albeit with scarcely a thought to the budgets the families had placed at her disposal. I have always noticed that rich people are pretty practical about budgets, and I imagine that there is the true secret of most of the world's fabulous fortunes.

The first thing she did was to rent one of the most imposing apartments in Dresden. If I remember rightly the building had been especially constructed for Augustus, elector of Saxony, about 1730, and it was as sumptuous as an apartment at Versailles.

When we were installed, groomed, trained to walk haughtily, coyly, or demurely (as the occasion might demand), and schooled in the art of pleasing the young German noblemen, we "received," dressed like miniature queens.

We received practically the whole court of Saxony, and the

apartment of the American *mädchen* grew to be a very lively place, as you may imagine.

Now all this cost a great deal of money, and while Mrs. C. had been given plenty, our fairly simple California parents had not bargained for anything so regal as our chaperon was attempting, and the debts, consequently, began to pile up to quite considerable sums.

Still it went on. I remember that in the daytime when lessons were to be done I dressed in simple middy blouses and wore pigtails, but when night came I became a very grown-up little lady with my long hair done up into a series of coils that ran three times round my head and let short little curls fall coquettishly at the back. You can see this monstrosity of a coiffure in the old German prints of the day, but you can imagine that I was very proud of it.

The climax of my Dresden schooling was being presented at court. Custom was that one had to be at least twenty-one years old, and I was in my fourteenth year. However this difficulty was easily overcome by the help of a Paris couturier (brought to Dresden at incredible cost, you may be sure) coiffeurs and specialists in "maquillage," and I was made to look like something between a wax doll and Catherine of Russia in full array. The train of my court dress was wonderfully long and wonderfully hard to manage, but Mrs. C., for all her economic weaknesses, knew her business when it came to training us, and so the Great Day passed without mishap, and we all graduated from childhood into the estate of *grandes dames* in the royal presence of the King and Queen of Saxony.

Then I fell in love.

The subject (or is it object?) of my first and girlish passion was a certain German prince who had the handsomest uniform in the world, the most romantic saber-scars on his most noble, though rather pink, face, the most fascinating way of stiffening and clicking his heels together when he saluted you (they all had this, naturally, but none seemed quite so perfect as he), and the most wonderfully rakish manner of saying ponderous German compliments I have ever listened to.

Oh yes, we became engaged. It was very formal, but very short-lived. I think it lasted a month. I loved him for his uniform, and even for the absurd gambling debts he had, and the terrible reputation he enjoyed (naturally I was sure he never had been really understood), but when I discovered one day that he had paid the equivalent of one hundred dollars for the handsome kid boots he wore, my good old California hardihood and sense of proportion got the better of me, and I broke it off with appropriate dignity.

I recall that he did not commit suicide.

It was a pretty close shave! I might have started life by being a princess in comic opera.

But just about that time Mrs. C. did something that altered our whole situation. She vanished.

She had spent all our money and used up all the patience of all the tradesmen in Dresden with her reckless debts. We had noticed vaguely that she was very nervous and excited, even irritable, but we did not give it much thought. One fine morning, however, we awoke to the fact that our jolly chaperon had packed her bags during the night and absconded, and furthermore, that we had nothing left in our luxurious apartment to pay the servants with or even to eat with. It was pretty mortifying and fairly tragic, but a cable to our collective parents brought temporary relief, and the very next boat brought several worried mothers to Germany.

Thus finished "finishing" in Dresden.

CHAPTER II

The Royal Palace of Madrid in Spain, during the 1890s.
Vintage engraving from Trousset encyclopedia, 1886–1891.

Now comes several months of cavorting about Europe, much or most of which is uninteresting. It is important, however, that my mother took me, among other places, to Madrid, for there I fell in love again.

This time it was quite a different sort of person from my German prince and his golden boots. The gentleman in question was a toreador. Perhaps not really a great matador (I seem to remember that he was the apprentice or perhaps the servant of one) but to me his greatness was simply enormous.

Most American girls of today will be "left cold," as they say, at the idea of a toreador. They have known their Valentinos and their Novarros (whether on the silver screen or in front of the local drug-store), but for a fifteen-year-old tomboy, removed from early Sacramento ranches only by a boat-ride and several yards of silk court-dress, a real live toreador (in the Eighties, too) complete with be-buttoned and be-ribboned and be-caped costume, was something to take away the breath.

This one took mine.

His name was Miguel. As nearly as I can remember him now he was handsome in that classical, long-eyed, swarthy, swaggering way that Spaniards are supposed to have and all affect. He was brutal, conceited, haughty, passionate, direct, childish and completely irresponsible. He was accustomed to getting . . . or taking . . . whatever he wanted. He wanted me, it seemed.

He had seen admiration in my eyes. He flashed his teeth at me and flourished a be-jeweled sombrero and waited for me to come to him. These are not quite the facts of the case but it amounted to that. My vanity prefers to leave the intimate details out of the story.

I came, all right. I made secret dates with him. I heard him through my ears, my eyes, my flesh, my pores . . . saying phrases that sent maggots into my brain, poured brimstone into my blood. In the same instant he could be my master or at my feet. His touch left scars on my soul. And when he kissed me, his breath proclaimed the fire that was to follow its vapor and bathed my body and heart in its madness while his hands gave off their electricity.

Well, we will not go into the details of my puppy love. Suffice it to say that my mother, who had a head on her shoulders, decided that we were going to England, and off we went, directly.

Just about time, too.

I learned, incidentally, that dear Miguel was killed in a *corrida* only a week after we left, so I suppose my tender and girlish nature was spared a real tragedy.

In London my aching heart was cured. It was a fairly brief process and a fairly odd one, and, although I never suspected it, it was to account later on for one of the most adventurous periods of my life. The man's name was David Kalakaua, and he was nothing less than king of the Hawaiian Islands.

Now you must not suppose that King Kalakaua was an ordinary savage, bedecked with beads and wearing fringe. On the contrary. He was quite a gentleman, even distinguished in a way, and had studied in the best schools of Britain, wore his cutaway or evening clothes with the best traditional air, and had a true gift of conversation (chiefly about himself and his fascinating country). He was childlike, too, in many ways, but that did not prevent him from becoming something of a rage among the bustled maidens of Victoria's court.

This was not a case of love, by the way. It was fascination, rather, that diverted my mind from the sway of my torrid toreador. I used to sit for hours and listen to tales of Hawaii, the costumes, the customs, the dances and the simple, natural life. It was the Finger of the East beckoning to me again.

And London in itself was a glorious adventure, for I was young enough and pretty enough . . . and rich enough . . . to be the object of attention of so many ardent young gentlemen that my little head was fairly turned.

But it was not to last.

My mother, with good common sense, decided that my European "education" had gone about far enough, and planned to take me back to San Francisco before I lost the strength and solidity of our own New World through the blandishments of the older and more sophisticated world. Or perhaps before I became the victim of some commercial, if amusing, gentleman who had dollar signs for eyes.

Back we went, and there ended my childhood altogether.

CHAPTER III

Sutter's Fort, Sacramento late 1800s.

I think the ruling passion of my life has been my love of contrasts. I remember reading somewhere ... probably nowhere of consequence ... a bit of philosophy that always impressed me as being the closest anybody has ever come to explaining the word "happiness." Vague as my memory is, the idea was this: It is not the *having* of things or people or experiences that gives happiness. It is the magic moment when your hand just closes on the thing. You may be bored or tired of it the very next moment, and so in order to keep on having the pleasure, you have to arrange for a whole series of getting ... an entire and very rapid series of closing your hand, so to speak.

No doubt I never could have thought that out for myself, not being philosophical, but that is just the way I feel. I think it explains very well, too, the way I lived.

Returning to California after being "finished" in Europe provided one of those contrasts. I did not want to return, but once on the boat, memories of the tomboy days in Sacramento by the filthy but wonderful water fronts came back to me vividly. So little Aimée Crocker left behind her the memories of shaven-headed German officers, red and yellow Spanish crowds, and ardent bullfighters, and the nice London Oxonians so correct in haberdashery and tonsorial art.

Contrasts grew. In Sacramento I lived on a ranch with cowboys, learned to ride anything on four legs, use a lariat and swear still better. In San Francisco I fell easily into the social life, had an apartment of my own (which I called a studio, Heaven knows why) and acted like a trained social seal. The experts my parents had paid to make me into this had done a good job.

That was my downfall.

I became engaged, secretly, to Porter Ashe.

He was the son of a prominent San Francisco family, very decent, very stubborn, and very much in love with me. And to make a long story short, we eloped and got ourselves married. I was just seventeen and he was twenty-one. A couple of young fools, may I add. The newspapers, always looking for some scandal or other, noticed that two scions of California families were rambling about together under an assumed name in a city where they did not belong. They caught us, and in order to avoid a nasty affair we had to confess ... and to prove, mind you ... the truth.

We were both in for parental rage. We both finally received parental blessings. And then we went on a real honeymoon, this time perfectly in the open.

We went to Los Angeles, and it was on this trip that I first met tragedy and death face to face. Our sleeper was attached to a train, part of which was a special to transport a large number of Chinese coolies. The train was overcrowded. We dined and retired for the night in our compartment, and we were thoroughly asleep when I awoke suddenly with the sensation of being in mid-air. The car was tipping forward and to the side. Then there was a terrible crash under me. I was thrown from my berth. I heard my husband cry out. Another grinding crash. The car rolled over. I was tossed about and bruised. Bodies fell on me. I still clung to my bedclothes and buried my head in them. Then there was a third terrific smash and the car seemed to crumple under me. Then I remembered nothing.

I came to. It was black night, but everything about me seemed to be glaring red and yellow light. Fire. I moved my hand and felt the broken splintered end of what had been a steel beam. I knew the car was burning. I heard cries and moaning about me. I dragged myself, dazed and frightened, to a sitting position, and then to my feet.

Flames were higher. Roaring and crackling. I found that I was standing, not upon the floor of the car, but upon the ground where the car had been turned over and was on its side, most of the woodwork having been torn away and the glass pulverized. I looked up and saw that the other side, too, was smashed, so that I could get through ... by climbing. I looked for my husband, but he was nowhere in sight, and the side of the compartment where his berth had been was a splintered mass of twisted wood and iron, lighted by the flames which now towered over the car.

My head ached, but I was otherwise unhurt as far as I could see. I started climbing. I heard men's voices outside, footsteps running, screams of pain. I succeeded in getting my head over the edge of what had been the other side (now overhead) and called out to some one who was running by. It was my husband. He had a handkerchief over his nose and had been unrecognizable, for the smoke was drawn down by the wind. He broke through and helped me to clamber up and over. It was high time.

I was able to draw back a little and see what had really happened. It was terrible. The entire train had left the track on the side of a mountain pass and had plunged down several hundred feet, telescoped and smashed six of the cars which now lay in flames, twisted and mangled like a huge broken snake.

But the last car, the one loaded with the coolies, had, strangely enough, rolled on its own wheels down the entire slope and, its speed checked by the underbrush and mud, had come to a stop at the bottom, unhurt, unscarred, unbroken, its entire charge of Celestials safe and sound.

I learned this later, but I could see the car down there, illuminated by the flames that burned the others.

Men and women crowded around me, most of them practically naked as I was myself save for the bedding to which I had instinctively clung. I was crying, too, I remember. I was not alone.

Bodies were being carried past us from further down.

Wrecking crew, local farmers, unharmed men amongst the passengers, even the despised Chinese coolies, were doing their best to recover the dead and injured from the burning wreck.

We were led back, up a difficult pass, to the railroad track where a flat car pushed by a dummy engine had rolled up. Shelter. The flat car was loaded with bodies, being piled up like lumber. The place was echoing with the moans of the injured and dying. It was insane, unbelievable, indescribable.

My husband, I learned about this time, had had a very narrow escape. He had been thrown through the window when the car turned over and had escaped being crushed to death by the other coaches only by a miracle. His face was fairly cut up by the glass of his window but there was nothing seriously wrong with him or with me either, for that matter.

There were, in all, forty-five killed and several hundred injured. Many were not then nor ever accounted for.

That was the famous wreck of Tahachapee Pass. A fine beginning for a honeymoon.

Honeymoon!

It was under a bad omen. I shall leave it and the consideration of my first marriage out of this book altogether. Let it suffice to say that we continued to Europe after recovering from the shock of the wreck and after staying a week in Los Angeles. But there was a jinx on us, despite the birth of my daughter and despite all that Husband Number One and I could do to make it go; it did not and could not last. I fled, so to speak, from Europe alone. My child arrived when I was in San Francisco. My divorce arrived soon after. And "Finis" was marked indelibly upon the first entry in my book of matrimony.

CHAPTER IV

Clipper Ship *Southern Cross* leaving America, by Fitz Hugh Lane.

‍‍‍‍‍‍~‍ ❧❦❧ ‍~

I s there anything so bewildering as a very young person who becomes, for one reason or another, "fed up with life"? One reads in the newspapers of youngsters who commit suicide just because their schoolmarks were not up to what they thought their parents expected of them, or because Mamma would not let Minnie go out with Eddy after ten P.M., or else because Papa refused to let Reginald, aged seventeen, wear the paternal dinner jacket to the High School Prom. Fed up. Disillusioned. Tired of this life. Some run away. Others try veronal. It all amounts to the same thing.

Well, my case was a little like that. It was in the same spirit that I made up my mind that I was through with the people of my world and with "civilized" life, for all time. I would go away into the green, natural places where men are men and women are all Hula-hula girls, and live my own life.

In short, I would go to the South Seas.

It was the call of the East: I did not know it then, but I was listening attentively to that spell. My plan was to be alone, to do everything alone, to be independent, not to have anybody to criticize nor to make suggestions. Here was I, a young divorced woman (very young and just barely divorced) and with an independent income, and why should I not? My imagination was on fire.

But where first?

I remembered the stories I had heard in London from King David Kalakaua, dapper monarch of the Sandwich Islands, better known as Hawaii. And the more I remembered, the more I became decided. Kalakaua had invited me himself. He had even urged me to come. So I determined to become one of those lotus-eaters who fed upon the fruits of that beautiful country and upon the beauty of solitary thought.

After winning a rather Pyrrhic victory over my ardently protesting parents, I set about finding a ship.

My advertisement in the San Francisco newspapers brought in a collection of replies that would make a good story in themselves had I the time to write it. Every sort of sailing vessel you can imagine was available and offered. Barques, brigantines, sloops, clippers, complete with crew, willing to do anything from copra trading to piracy.

But only one interested me.

In large, breezy, wispy, flowing hand came a letter, signed "Ephraim Judd (Captain)," who described his seventy-foot schooner, *Tropic Star*, as being the "trimmest and seaworthiest little craft that ever sailed the Pacific. And, Madam, she is at your service provided only that you are not a missionary. Her last service was missionaries and the crew will not stand for no more of them, so I ask you, Madam, to be frank with me on this score, if it please you, Madam."

A missionary ship!

Amused, I wrote him and made an appointment. The *Tropic Star* turned out to be all he claimed for her. She was a little slow, perhaps, but seaworthy and comfortable and in excellent condition. The crew, with the exception of the first mate,

Mr. Dow, were a mixture of Kanakas, Scandinavians, negroes and less definite races, totaling ten. Mr. Dow was an American from New Bedford, and he was the official strong man of the ship. There was also a Chinese cook, called Sam, who had learned to smile when he was very young and practiced it perpetually.

Having reassured Captain Judd that I had no interest in saving the souls of savages or of anybody else, and that as far as I was concerned there would be no gospel preaching aboard, we bargained for a year's charter of the *Tropic Star* to a point where I was only slightly cheated, and the trip was definitely planned.

Our immediate destination was Honolulu: after that ... anywhere in the world. We got off, I being the only passenger, amid the earnest warnings and tearful misgivings of family and friends, and soon the Golden Gate was vanishing behind our wake. The voyage was totally uneventful, barring a storm that gave me a glorious thrill when I recovered from my first fear, a shark which we harpooned and hauled over the side, and one single incident which is worth telling.

Mr. Dow, as I have said, was the strong man of the ship. He was a silent, hard-faced, thin-lipped man of forty or thereabouts. He was of only medium height, but he had the broadest shoulders and the deepest chest I have ever seen on a human being, whatever his race. I also remember that he had a perpetual scrubby growth of black whiskers, as though he forgot to shave more than once a week, and that his eyes, very far apart, hidden under thick shaggy eyebrows, seemed to be triangular. I have since noticed that prize-fighters have similar eyes. Perhaps it is the sign of a certain instinct.

At all events, Mr. Dow was very much respected, if not liked, by the crew. His orders were crisp, brief, and issued without profanity. The men obeyed him with more alacrity than they did Captain Judd, who was just a lovable old fellow with white hair and a Cape Cod beard.

But there was one man in the forecastle called Sully ... I do not know whether it was short for Sullivan (he did have red hair) or whether that was his right name ... and he was a trouble-maker. Also a bad sailor, I was informed later, and I could see it, too.

But Sully was a giant. He stood well over six-foot-three and was built in proportion. The only job he seemed to do with any sign of willingness was to swab down the deck. Then he could strip to the waist and exhibit his magnificent torso, his bulging muscles and his Herculean arms, all bristling with ruddy hair that gave him something of the appearance of a huge pink gorilla.

From the first day it was easy to see that no love was lost between Mr. Dow and Sully. Not that the mate showed open dislike or that Sully refused to carry out orders, but there was a sort of shuffling swagger that the red man put on whenever he received one, and there was a peculiar metallic quality in Mr. Dow's voice whenever he had occasion to speak to the other.

One day I got up very early in the morning to see the sea at dawn. The men were busy swabbing down. Sully, his big body glistening with sea-mist, was making chests to impress his shipmates while he worked. He saw me as I came up on deck, and he turned straight at me. He leered, dropped his mop and flexed his bulging biceps and breast muscles the way strong men do in vaudeville shows. I might have admired it, too, but I did not like his conceited leer, and so I turned my back on him and crossed the deck.

Suddenly I heard a sharp word.

Mr. Dow had appeared from nowhere and had ordered the man back to work. They stood there for a minute, looking at each other. I could see real animal hatred in Sully's face. Then, when Mr. Dow turned away with his quiet dignity, Sully made a disgusting, insulting noise with his lips. The First Mate turned like a flash. He stepped up to the towering giant and said something in a low voice, got an answer which I will not repeat here, and with one blow knocked the big man down.

What happened then came so fast that I can only remember the high spots. Sully was on his feet again in a fraction of a second and leaped at the First Mate like a tiger, his great red hands clutching, his face and his whole body as red as his hair, completely transformed into a brute.

As the man reached for him, Mr. Dow stepped aside and hit him three terrific blows. I thought it would have killed anybody else. Then they went at it, toe to toe. I cannot describe it, but I have never seen two human beings in my life so completely changed. I caught a glimpse of Mr. Dow's face, and I knew right then that the only thought in his mind was to kill the man in front of him.

He very nearly did it, too. Hitting with a power that still seems unbelievable to me, even today after I have seen many a professional fighter in the ring, he knocked the huge fellow down again and again, and when the red man had had apparently enough for all his big torso and muscles, the mate picked him up, and standing him there groggily, smashed him in the face so that the blood spurted out. Sully fell down unconscious, but Mr. Dow was not finished. Still raging, he picked up the big red body again and threw it against a stanchion and would have done so again if one of the men had not tried to hold him back, pointing to me standing there.

The mate turned his tiger's face towards me blankly, then drew himself together and said:

"Sorry."

That was all. He walked away, controlled once more, with that usual poise and quiet dignity of his.

Sully went on the sick list for the rest of the trip. I learned that his jaw-bone was broken, two ribs cracked and his nose completely smashed. I understood then something of our mate's authority.

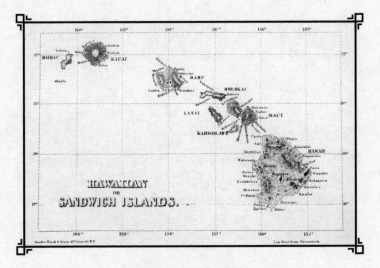

CHAPTER V

Map of Hawaii or the Sandwich Islands, *c.* 1854.

B ut our voyage ended.

Honolulu.

Diamond Head, sticking proudly up over us, a mountain rock, the blue harbor, the palms, little brown bodies swimming out to the schooner as she tacked into the basin. Strange-looking craft darting about us, paddled by more little brown people. Cries like songs. Far away somewhere a drum or some percussion instrument beating a rhythmic tum-tum-tum-tum.

No factories on the horizon. No storage docks. No industry. No smoke-cloud. No hum of machines. No rancid smells. No industrial waste afloat. No city skyline. Little houses over the water on poles. Hundreds of children playing on a magnificent beach, untouched by picnic parties and unstrewn with their banana peels.

That is the first impression I had of the East ... for it is the fringe of the East ... the mid-ocean doorway to the East. I have been back to Honolulu more than once since the entry of American industrialism into the affairs of Hawaii, and I have felt a sense of being hurt. I have had a sense of being deprived of something. But it is still beautiful; you cannot destroy so perfect and so powerful a beauty. But the great simplicity, the freshness of that pearl-like cluster of islands is gone, fled before the march of missionaries, Marines and modernity.

Now it is one thing to be received at a European court in your overlong robes, but a distinctly different thing to be greeted by the ruler of an island full of sweet but semi-civilized people, all of whom are born and remain good and generous and lovable, but distinctly untaught in the magnificent ways of the West.

The Palace of King David Kalakaua was not any ramshackle bamboo affair as you might imagine, however. It was an immense modern stone building, and a very beautiful practical thing, too. My confusion came when I was greeted by innumerable dignitaries in decent white suits . . . and bare feet.

There was absolutely no self-consciousness about them, for all their lack of shoes, and they were very considerate and courteous. Some of them spoke something that I recognized, vaguely, as English, and I made it known that I had come to see their king.

The idea penetrated eventually, and a little later my friend David Kalakaua appeared, very splendid in whites . . . and complete with shoes, too. Probably no one in the world has ever been as surprised as he to see the little girl he had spun yarns to a few years ago in London, all grown up and arriving, unannounced, on the grand porch of his Palace. But he contained himself with proper dignity, for there were formalities to be gone through with, and he made a long speech in Hawaiian to the assembled crowd which had gathered at my arrival. It was a very beautiful speech, although I understood not a word, and it made me fall immediately in love with his language. I learned later that Hawaiian utilizes very few consonants, and certainly to the ear it seems like a liquid flow of vowels. I have often wished I could hear "Die Valkyrie" or "Parsifal" in Hawaiian.

When the formalities were over, we ... (Captain Judd, Mr. Dow, and I, that is) ... were brought into the Palace, and it was amusing to see the Island manner of our king change for that of a London drawing-room.

We were presented to the Queen, one of the most charming women I have ever met, whose native name was Kapiolani, and her younger sister Liki-Liki, and we were made to feel at home in real earnest.

How long would we stay? An American house was mine if I would please to take it. (It turned out to be a portable affair, delivered by Sears, Roebuck and Co.) Or would I prefer to stay at the hotel?

All these and a hundred more questions were asked, and I must admit that King David Kalakaua was more than pleased as well as surprised to learn that I had no time limit on my visit. Here was real hospitality and no selfish pretense of it.

An amusing incident marked the afternoon. The King had imported or brought back with him from London one hundred and five Royal Guards, with all their trappings. These he intended to use for parade purposes on special occasions. And my arrival gave him his first such "special occasion," so the Palace guards were duly dressed up for a great demonstration.

Ceremonies started toward three o'clock. The men, gleaming and gorgeous and gaudy and very marvelous indeed, marched past the Palace and through the town, under the command of five officers (of whatever rank: I think they were all generals) more or less in step.

But when they returned to the Plaza in front of the Palace,

every last man of them, officers included, was stripped naked save for the usual loin-cloth, and was carrying the precious British uniform and furry shako behind him.

In a temperature of 93 degrees Fahrenheit it is difficult to be military, let alone to be British. Even the King had a good laugh over it, albeit the joke was really on him.

CHAPTER VI

King Kalakaua of Hawaii, 1882. Hawaii State Archives.

It would be impossible to give any sort of a day-to-day account of my life in Hawaii, not only because my memory of it is dimmed and distorted, but especially because it may not be very interesting when told that way. What I want to do is to give a general impression of life in pre-American Hawaii and to touch some of the higher spots. As a matter of fact there are several hundred books on the Sandwich Islands, past and present, and it is not my purpose to compete with globe-trotting writers of travelogues. And I have been told by my friends that, for a person who had traveled as much as I have, I retain less of the obvious things and more of the *underneath* things than anybody they know.

At any rate my life began very newly in the Hawaiian Islands. Most of my time was devoted to riding and swimming. Incidentally I was fairly good at both sports. This last sentence recalls two interesting things, too, and I shall put them down here before I let them slip by me.

The first concerns a horse named "Monte Carlo." I had bought him to enter the weekly races which the King patronized and sponsored, and I learned to love him very much.

When I purchased Monte Carlo I was warned that he was very dangerous except with those whom he happened to like, and that he liked very few persons. Well, he got to like me, it seems, for he was as docile and sweet as could be, and he won several races for me, sometimes riding him myself and other times with a little Hawaiian boy up that I trained to jockey him.

But when I finally decided to leave the Island and to sail on to the South Seas, an American woman who lived rather mysteriously (she was really a sort of demimondaine who had exiled herself from San Francisco for reasons best known to herself) wanted to buy him.

Now I wanted to send Monte Carlo home to my Sacramento ranch, really, and I told the woman about his peculiar disposition, hoping to scare her off. Not a chance. She insisted, and, realizing that it would be more practical to sell him than to send him back to the continent, I let her have her way.

I sailed away toward adventures that you will hear of later on, and when I came back to Hawaii I learned that the first time she rode him he carried her calmly enough to the open road, and that then, without warning or apparent reason he dumped her off and walked on her with all fours. She was killed instantly while some natives looked on, powerless to interfere.

The second incident was a swimming adventure, and includes one of the greatest scares I have ever had.

The bay upon which Waikiki Beach gives is supposed to be free from sharks. This is largely true because of the shallows at the mouth of the Bay and because of some peculiar construction of the bottom (I do not understand these technical things very well). Everybody swims there, and frequently we swam at night, going in from the King's beautiful boathouse pier. The water was always at perfect temperature, the air always warm, night or day, and the picture of the beach as you look back, floating or swimming, with its torches and Chinese lanterns, was really beautiful.

One day I went in with a bathing-party consisting of King David Kalakaua, some members of his Court, and some of the dancing-girls from the Palace.

I was a fairly strong swimmer and I got ahead of the party, paddling about not far from the narrows where the bay proper begins.

Suddenly I felt something under me. It was just as if some person were playing a prank, and, swimming under water, had come up under me, lifting me high on his back. I was lifted, in fact, quite out of the water. I laughed at first, but when the swimmer did not reappear I began to have misgivings and swam back to the group as fast as ever I could. When I told them my story. everybody began to swim in hard, and they assured me that I had made the acquaintance of a shark. There was no more swimming that evening, and everyone was very careful for days. It seems that if it were really true about it being a shark and not some other big fish or turtle, I was more than lucky not to have been cut by his dorsal fin, perhaps even seriously mutilated or killed.

King Kalakaua thought it must have been a very small shark, for, as he himself said, "A man-eater would have made more of an impression." I was just as glad.

One thing that perhaps people do not know is that sharks are supposed to prefer white human flesh to brown. Many of the European and American visitors to Hawaii in those days used to swim in black tights and jerseys that covered almost all their bodies, so that the sharks, if any, would mistake them for natives. This may be just a superstition, but it seemed to work, for we had no casualties . . . except one.

That one was Mr. Dow, my strong-armed mate.

The death of the mate is one of the most pathetic stories I know. It was a real fatality. I did not witness it myself, thank God, but what I did see of it was enough.

Mr. Dow, as you may have imagined, was a daring and powerful swimmer, belying completely the legend that sailors are at home on, but not in, the water. He also wore a charm-amulet that had been given him by an Indian sorcerer from some part of the South American coast. Whether it worked or not is not the story. The fact is that he swam far out very often, past the narrows, to the reef where Kalipi Creek met the sea, easily and slowly, like a machine. Nothing ever happened to him, regardless of the many warnings of the natives, and he had a perfect confidence in the powers of his amulet over the tiger-like sharks of the outside deep water.

Now there was a little Kanaka girl called Pali-Mana who loved Mr. Dow. She would follow him around wherever he went, keeping some distance in back of him, timidly, but radiating admiration for the sturdy sailor. At first he was embarrassed, then he began to like it. He ended by "marrying" her in the native ceremony, and she lived with him in the Sears, Roebuck house (which I had evacuated, meantime, in favor of a more primitive, native one of grass).

Pali-Mana was fascinated by Mr. Dow's amulet. She wanted it and asked him for it, time and again, but he very firmly and seriously refused to give it to her. It got to be quite a joke on the island.

One day when they were both lazing on the beach he fell asleep, and the mischievous Pali-Mana slipped it off his neck, put it around her own, and started swimming out, calling to everybody within hearing that she had at last stolen the magic charm.

When he awoke, a few minutes afterwards, he missed his wife and his amulet. Some of the crowd called laughingly out to him, and he saw the delighted gesticulations of Pali-Mana, some hundred yards out in the bay. He easily guessed what had happened.

Rather annoyed by her prank, he plunged in after her, and a swimming race ensued, while all the beach watched, amusedly. Pali-Mana, like all the native girls, was a fish in the water and the powerful strokes of Mr. Dow were not more than enough to catch her after a serious struggle. Out and out they swam, past Mokulo Island, nearing the inlet constantly, until, little by little, the girl began to tire and the great strength of the American began to tell.

Then suddenly, while everyone watched from along the beach, far back, something happened. There was a flicker of water near Mr. Dow. His powerful voice screamed ... (that is the only word I have for it: I was not there, but I was told about it right afterwards) ... and everybody knew that tragedy had happened.

Pali-Mana swam furiously back towards her man, who had stopped swimming and seemed to be sinking. Rapid little canoes pushed off from the shore. The girl, insane with fear for her husband, was screaming and calling.

And when the unconscious American seaman was finally brought in, his leg had been cut off short at the thigh, almost as if shorn by a knife. Every effort was made to save him, but he died three days later from loss of blood, and Pali-Mana, inconsolable, disappeared one morning never to be seen again.

So much for the superstition of the amulet. One does not attempt to explain these things. In the East you learn to accept. You do not apply Western logic to that which you see but do not understand.

CHAPTER VII

A missionary preaching to the natives under a screen made of plaited cocoa-nut leaves at Kairua by William Ellis.

M y time in Hawaii was troubled only by one thing. Perhaps the word "troubled" is badly chosen, but I might truly have been annoyed had I been more thin-skinned ... or if I had cared.

The trouble was missionaries.

Now I am perfectly aware that there have been and are good, earnest, well-working missionaries who are content to let human beings be human, and occupy themselves only with the spirit and the welfare of those whom they have gone out to teach. But one thing I do know is that many of those who came to Hawaii in those early days only brought trouble and harm, and many others enriched themselves at the expense of the honest, good little people they had come there to convert to the creed of Christ.

All that aside, and call it injured pride if you want to, the missionaries were no friends of mine on the island. In the first place I scandalized them, and they criticized me for the way I lived. I have become used to that: others than missionaries have criticized my way of living and have been scandalized at me during my life.

But the things they objected to were so silly. Just because I refused to live like an American or the way most of the handful of white persons on the island did, and that I knew and liked many of the dancing-girls, dressed as they did when I wanted to, and learned to dance the hula-hula (not the cheap thing of the modern vaudeville stages and night-clubs, thank you) and that I generally had a good time in my own and really harmless way, they were distressed and harassed and annoyed beyond measure. And these ladies and gentlemen of suppressed desires and ill-gained possessions first complained to the King.

He sent them about their business with a word of warning. Kalakaua hated the missionaries, for they stirred trouble among his subjects and undid most of his own good work with their stupidly mistaken ideas that the natives should live like the residents of Detroit or Kalamazoo.

Then one day they sent a deputation to me and accused me of being an "immoral hussy" or words to that effect, because I had "sunken to the level of the aborigines." It appears that they felt I was setting a bad example to the natives they were trying to convert by not acting superior to them. In short they asked me . . . commanded me, rather . . . to leave the Islands.

But it did not work.

And because I preferred to remain and continue to enjoy myself, they sent glowing, but unfair, accounts of my life and doings to the San Francisco papers, the only effect of which was to distress my perfectly innocent parents and friends, although the scandal stories did make pretty good reading. I almost wish they had been true.

Well, if by refusing to snub and patronize the natives we did them harm, I wonder how these good, commercial men-of-God will answer one day for the land and property they took away from the Kanakas. For instance, they would lend money against the signature or mark of some unsuspecting and completely ignorant Hawaiian who wanted to build a house or something, and when the year or whatever period was up, he quite naturally could not pay, and the representative of Heaven would simply place his own value on the property and take it over for himself. Kanakas are, by nature, improvident. Child-like and happy, they have a carefree disregard of anything that we might call commercial and when their property was taken away from them by "divine right" they were totally bewildered and understood nothing about it at all, but gave in to the superior authority of the white men.

If missionaries only could recognize that there is no poverty until you tell some one he is poor, no sin until you label it, the work of soul-saving would be a better work, and uplifting a thing truly noble. All the Kanakas were and still are born good. They are loving, natural, animal . . . what you like, but good and generous. They had their own codes, their own tabus and laws. Crimes such as are all too frequent in our Western civilization were unknown, save for the natural instances where a death paid for a death, and very little of that. There was no immorality because there was no moral code. It was, for instance, perfectly natural for the Hawaiian to take to himself the woman he wanted . . . under the provision of his own laws and customs.

Came the missionaries. They set up standards which may be all very well to govern the lives of citizens of Ohio, but have nothing whatever to do with the inhabitants of an island in the middle of the Pacific. Under the guise of decency and sanitation they taught that nakedness was indecent and unsanitary. The national dance, the hula-hula, they called carnal and filthy.

I understand that it has now been forbidden by the American administrators.

Result of this? Natives have become sex-conscious, body-conscious, law-conscious, and conscious of everything that makes life in industrialized European and American cities so tawdry, so rotten underneath.

Missionaries! Rubbish! If there is a God ... a personal God such as those Christian meddlers and busybodies teach about ... it is fairly sure that the simple goodness of the Hawaiians must have been very pleasing to Him. Are we not a little cocksure, a little conceited, in thinking that we only, who have specialized our lives to be in tune with automobiles, radios, cinemas ... (and our drunkenness and organized crimes and white-slavery, by the way) ... are the only ones upon whom the Divine Eye looks with favor?

But King David Kalakaua had his revenge on the missionaries, and it was rather amusing.

He gave an official ball. He commanded ... commanded, mind you, as a king and absolute ruler the missionaries of both sexes to attend. They came, for it would have been impolite to refuse. Kalakaua and I led the dance under their very noses, I clad in native costume (rather, more or less unclad, according to their ways of thinking) and danced with the Palace dancing-girls to the applause of the King and Queen Kapiolani.

Now to understand this you should know that an official dance in Hawaii in those days got to be something of an orgy. The music, the rustle of the "grass" skirts, the rhythm of the drums ... and the drinking of *ava* (a sort of intoxicating drink made from a root and extracted by chewing, spitting and distilling, which I never had the stomach to try) ... not to mention gin which the Americans themselves imported ... had a definitely sensual effect both upon the men and the women. The result must have been pretty shocking to the American missionaries who believe (or so pretend) that sex is a fundamental sin instead of a pleasant and perfectly natural instinct.

At all events, there they sat, all through it. I remember the look on their faces, the hypocrites. I will wager that that group never forgot that night, for one reason or another.

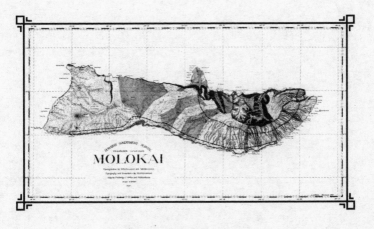

CHAPTER VIII

The island of Molokai, Land Office Map, 1897.

In some ways I would like to go on with a lot of description about Hawaii and include many little stories and anecdotes which might be readable but which really have nothing to do with the general plan of this book. But I am afraid I will have to leave that for the geographers and travel-writers while I go on to other things.

Nevertheless I want to mention the revolution. I ought to write "Revolution." And I must not forget Molokai, the island of lepers, and at least one adventure there.

David Kalakaua, king of the Hawaiian or Sandwich Islands, was a good man but perhaps a bad monarch. That is to say that he was out of touch with his time. He had feudalistic rather than republican leanings.

That little note of history which stamps Hawaii as one of the first kingdoms on record to adopt the constitutional form of government is scarcely remembered by the world, but it is a fact. David Kalakaua was chosen by popular vote to be king of his people. These people were good people, as I have said. Even their national motto, "*Ua Man Ke ea o ka aina i ka pono,*" reflects it. It means "The life of the land is made longer through goodness." Long savage, those people have tried to become modern. And when their king, their chosen ruler, tried to force upon them a government which would give him a less limited authority than their constitution granted, they rebelled.

It was a revolution. Not a revolution such as the war for American independence or the blood-stained days of Robespierre and Danton in France. There was no bloodshed, no great upheaval. There was merely a demonstration during which the people stated their intentions ... whilst the King was swimming at Waikiki Beach.

I remember it very well, for I was in the bathing party. A large crowd of natives had gathered on the beach, and the king came up onto the deck of his boathouse and said gravely:

"It appears there is a revolution. There will be a new constitution tomorrow." And then he plunged in again.

There was, in fact, a new constitution which limited his power even more than was expected, but I know very little about those or any other politics. One thing I do remember, however, and that was something that the King was very proud of. It seems that he was responsible for a free-trade treaty with the United States, and as such he is written down in Hawaiian history as one of the great rulers of the Islands.

David Kalakaua died in 1891. He was visiting in San Francisco at the time, and he had attended a dinner in his honor at my home, only a few days before his death. A good man and a good friend.

The story of Molokai and the leper colony takes me back to before that time, however. There are really two stories, one of which happened some time later when I visited Hawaii again.

To begin with, I had been given an island near Molokai and I became princess and ruler of the three hundred people who lived on it ... not lepers, thank you. This was all through the kindness of King David, and it included a ceremony in which I was given a Hawaiian name, Palaikalani, which means "Bliss of Heaven." I did no actual ruling, of course, but I made frequent visits to "my" island, and "my" people were very sweet and amusing.

It was on one of those visits that King Kalakaua proposed a visit to the leper colony at Molokai, for it seems he made an official call there every year. I went with him and the royal party, and, while I do not want to be depressing nor describe in detail the horrors of that place, I do want to say, for the glory of the old Hawaiian government in the pre-American days, that the colony was a clean, immaculately maintained, up-to-date institution.

My visit to Molokai had a curious aspect. Far less was known of leprosy in those days, and in the twentieth century science seems to have proven that it is not the horror legends and ignorance have painted it. But in the 1880s it was considered so virulent and contagious that danger was supposed to exist even in passing near to anyone afflicted.

Consequently we went to all possible lengths to avoid contagion, even to the point of putting on special clothes of rubber that covered us from head to foot, and completed the outfit with rubber gloves and heavy veils. Today doctors tell me this was absurd, but all these precautions impressed me, as you can imagine, and I still have the feeling that it was better so.

The lepers, and especially the women, fascinated me, not only in a morbid way, but really. In the first place they were very beautiful. In the early stages of the disease the skin becomes gloriously silky and smooth and rich and white and it is truly wonderful to see. Then there was the strange psychology of the victims. They had a peculiar self-consciousness: it seemed to have taken possession of them in a way almost brutal. They were obsessed with a desire to touch with their hands anyone who was "clean," who was not afflicted as they were. It was because of this that the yearly visits the King made to Molokai were considered so very dangerous. Nowadays we know, or so we are told by science, that the touch is not contagious, but I, for one, would not feel pleasant even now to shake hands with one of those I saw there.

Many of the leper colony were not at all diseased, and that was a strange thing. I remember that there was one American man there who was married to a leper woman, a native, and suffered no consequences at all. I had a chance to speak with him, and asked him how he could possibly live there, let alone marry such a woman. He seemed a little bewildered at my question, and it was apparent that he saw nothing at all out of the way in either his life or his marriage. King David told me afterwards that this was the third leprous wife the American had had, and that his children ... there were four of them ... were as clean and untouched as any other children anywhere. It seemed pretty incongruous to me, but in the light of modern study I suppose it was not phenomenal at all.

Depressing as Molokai certainly was, the inhabitants were so resigned to their fate that they, apparently, did not notice that side of it. At least they spent no time in mourning or in sadness. I personally witnessed a dance ... called a ball, naturally ... in the great common-room of the main hospital, at which not only all the dancers but all the musicians were lepers. The King's party stood behind glass partitions and we watched for some time, fascinated. If there was any difference between these sick people and the rest of the world it seemed that they enjoyed themselves more simply.

At any rate it was a far cry from the lepers of the Bible or the Crusades with their clack-dishes and their mournful cry of "Unclean, unclean!"

But I have another story to tell about lepers which is more dramatic and less descriptive. It did not happen during my first visit to Hawaii but several years later when I came again with my third husband. However I will tell it here because in this book I shall not mention the Islands again.

To begin with there was a very strange man in Honolulu who had come, nobody knew why, and had taken residence there. His name was Washington Irving Bishop.

Picture him as the ugliest, most misshapen, most repulsive, and at the same time most attractive man in the world. There are, as you know, some people who are so repulsive that they fascinate you. That was his type.

Bishop was a hypnotist, both by preference and by profession. He had earned for himself a considerable reputation in America and had made a great deal of money on the vaudeville stage. For obscure, and probably not very tellable reasons, he had come to Hawaii, and was held there by the lazy, beautiful, enervating life, a hypnotic more powerful than his own.

One day, when we had gone to the hotel in Honolulu to see Bishop give a "seance" demonstrating his powers, I made his acquaintance ... to my later regret. My first sight of the man sickened me. He was scarcely more than a dwarf, had a large cadaverous face that was pitted with pock-marks and yellow as old parchment. His hands were too large, his arms too long, and even in his evening clothes he gave the impression of something inhuman and horrid. His eyes especially were extraordinary, and from them seemed to radiate . . . a force, a presence.

Well, his public "seance" was not only interesting but convincing. It was very evident that he was, at least, no fake, and the most skeptical people in the audience were entirely satisfied. He was able to dominate the wills of his subjects by placing them in a state of catalepsy, and in that state he made them do anything he wished.

Now things like that are and always have been my weakness. And when Bishop asked for volunteers from the audience, I responded almost without knowing it, and went up to the platform. I do not know why I did it. It seemed perfectly natural for me. Some of my friends laughed at me and some were shocked.

I can still remember the little grotesque man standing in front of me, peering from under his bushy eyebrows. I can remember how he lifted his hand and leered at me. I remember also that he was speaking to me quietly with his soft, rich voice . . . the only thing about him that could be called beautiful.

After that I remember nothing at all. What I write now was told me later. Apparently I sang and did silly things, much to the amusement of the spectators and to the complete disgust of my friends. But the important thing is that when I went down from the platform, this man-monster, this ugly, out-of-shape man who had so thoroughly disgusted me, had become, in my changed mind, the most fascinating creature in the world.

I talked with Washington Irving Bishop after the performance for several hours. He promised to teach me something of hypnotism, assuring me that I had a definite tendency towards his powers. He promised to do this privately . . . for a consideration.

The upshot was that I began to study with this curious man, and this resulted in an infatuation which was to go on for several weeks. I am not, I may say, very proud of it.

As a matter of fact, Bishop was a clever, brilliant man who might have been really great, but managed to be just a swine. The use he made of his power and his knowledge of human psychology, aside from the financial consideration, was cowardly and caddish. We will not go into that other than to say that he managed, fantastically enough, to make himself absolutely irresistible to women.

When I say that there was not a woman in the world whom, if he had desired her, he could not have had, it is nothing but the truth. The best example of this happened right in the hotel in Honolulu when the wife of a young naval officer, a very fastidious and rather snobbish sort of woman, commented on his leering, disgustingly conceited manner, quite loudly enough for him to hear.

"Well," she said, "I think the Americans on this Island have pretty bad taste to tolerate this ape-man and to stand for his insolent manners."

That remark was her doom.

Bishop turned to the man who happened to be standing beside him, unabashed and not the least bit troubled by this insult, and said:

"So? Well this is where Beauty gets carried off by the Beast. Wait and see what our finicky lady thinks of the 'ape' in about ten minutes."

Then he fixed his eyes on her for five minutes or so.

She did not look at him, but she grew fidgety and nervous. Finally she turned around and looked squarely at him, curiously and a little frightened. Then she drew herself up and looked coldly away from him. But it was only to turn around again in a little while. Then suddenly she left the people she was talking with and came over to Bishop. They talked for a short time, and then he turned to the company and said in his leering way:

"Gentlemen, good night."

They left together.

In three days there was a nasty scandal. He caused it purposely, although he could have protected her if he had wanted to. Four days later she killed herself with veronal.

Now all this seems quite a long way from leprosy, which was the excuse for this story, but right here is about where it comes in.

My acquaintance ... I was about to say, my friendship ... with Bishop, grew rapidly. The pure idea of hypnotism fascinated me. The fact that I could be brought out of myself and could drift, through his influence, into another sort of existence, was like the realization of a dream. And even the man himself bewildered me and fascinated me beyond my control.

Husband Number Three did not share my enthusiasm for Washington Irving Bishop, as you may have already divined, and he asked me to drop him before I should involve myself in the same sort of scandal that had already fastened itself on the names of other women. Like a silly girl with a new toy, I did not want to, but when I found that my husband was so very much in earnest I gave in and grew rather cold towards my gallant hypnotist.

Result: unpleasant scenes and quarrels with Bishop.

Finally he became so annoying that I was perfectly glad on

my own behalf to drop him, and I told him so. His reply is no matter, but when the storm was over he asked me very sweetly, almost tearfully, for a rendezvous in a beautiful grove near the old Royal Hawaiian Hotel. I agreed, believing it would be the easiest way out, and I told him it would be the last time I would see him.

He met me, and he had a horse and buggy there. We drove out through the country towards the south of Honolulu city. About three miles away there was a bleak hospital building surrounded with an iron fence. At the gate he stopped the horse and said something to the attendant, who let us in. I do not recall exactly what explanation he gave me for coming there, but it was something to do with his experiments in psychology, I think. At any rate, I was quite used to queer things from Bishop, and thought very little of it. I let him lead me, especially as I felt I had really hurt him that morning. But in a few minutes I was to learn just how devilish a human being can be.

Walking down the ash-covered road that led to the hospital, I noticed some men running towards us. As one approached I saw, to my horror, that his ears were swollen and distorted and hung down as far as his shoulders. He was a leper in the advanced stages. There was a strange quality . . . scarcely to be described as a look . . . a mad sort of quality, which I can still hardly describe without emotion. His hands were reaching out at us . . . at me. His lips, all moldy, were distended. His mouth, scarred and withered and blanched with disease, was crying out . . . and although I did not understand, I knew that it was to me he was calling.

Now I am not timid, not easily frightened, but the terror I knew at that moment is more than I can write. As for my "friend" Bishop, his true character, the depth of his fiendishness, became apparent then.

Instead of standing between me and the mad leper, as a gentleman might have done, he held me in front of him, tightly in his arms, as though purposely to let me be contaminated with the foulest disease in the world. And there were still more inhabitants of the hospital running behind the first comer.

I guess I was pretty maniacal. I hardly remember what I said or did, but apparently I kicked wildly and caught Bishop in the sensitive shin bone so that he let go his hold for an instant. It was enough for me to wrench myself free, and I flew towards the gate and through, as fast as I could, and climbed into the buggy and whipped the horse.

Bishop ran after me, calling out that it was only a joke. But I had lost my sense of humor. I thought it was so "funny" that I laid the whiplash across his face and left him there to walk back while I drove the poor old hag at her best speed into town.

There ended, or almost ended, the account of my hypnotist flirt. Naturally I did not see him again, but the story of his death deserves telling, and I can think of no better place for it than right here.

It happened in New York, about two years after the incidents I have just described. My husband and I had come back to America after a trip to Japan and China, going over the ground I had played over all by myself ... which is another part of this book. We ended in New York ourselves, and we came in "at the mort," so to speak.

Bishop, it was reported in the papers, had been found dead. He had died in the Old Lambs Club after a dinner at which he had given some exhibition of his powers. They had come upon him apparently sleeping peacefully in an armchair. For some time he was not disturbed but finally a physician who had attended the dinner was called and he pronounced him dead. The police were notified and an autopsy performed.

At the coroner's inquest there were wild scenes and Bishop's mother, who had some of her son's talents, as well as being an opera singer, grew hysterical and shrieked that her son had been murdered. At Malta it seems that he had once been pronounced dead by several doctors when he was only insensible. The medical opinion was that he had died of a rare and peculiar disease, Hystero-Catalepsy. The coroner chided the doctors for their haste in performing the autopsy but the charge of murder was not pressed. All this commanded considerable space in the papers in the month of May 1889, particularly in *The New York Herald*.

Now Bishop was partly famous and certainly notorious, and was considered one of the most curious characters of his day. No provision for his burial had been provided for in his will, nor was his estate (some hundreds of thousands of ill-gained dollars) left to any heir. It was not, therefore, a difficult matter for the head surgeon of a certain hospital to obtain his body for experimental purposes. He ... that is, his body ... was taken to the laboratory and dissected. It was immediately discovered that he had been no more dead than you or I, but that he had been taken in a sort of trance, a cataleptic fit or suspended animation.

I happen to know that Bishop had practiced upon himself very often. His one great desire had always been to have his subconscious self develop a power great enough and controlled enough to bring himself out of such a trance. Well, that one time, at least, he failed and I suppose that is the only case on record of a human being having been cut to pieces on a dissecting table while he was alive. His end turned out to be as curious as his life.

If I were a vindictive woman I might say that it served him right.

CHAPTER IX

Diadem mountain at sunset, Tahiti by John La Farge. Brooklyn Museum.

he death of Bishop provides me with a good place to leave my overlong description of Hawaii and my memories of it, and to take you away from the Island with me in my good schooner, *Tropic Star*. My crew was more or less unchanged, save for Sully and the unfortunate Mr. Dow who was replaced by a stranded American named Coddy. Mr. Coddy was so thin that a self-respecting shark would never have bothered him except in a case of sea-famine.

We set sail in early June with Tahiti as our destination. The voyage was relatively uneventful, and before I relate the only incident that made our run a little less monotonous than most long sailing voyages, I wish to say that I will not go into a catalogue of the South Sea Island nor of Samoa, which we visited a little later, for fear of having too little interesting material or of seeming to compete with the many travel books one can read on the subject.

But there was one event on that voyage which is amusing.

It happened soon after our departure from Hawaii; about three days off, if I remember rightly.

Captain Judd and I were sitting aft over a friendly glass, and the good old sailor was telling me some of his earlier adventures as a whaler.

Suddenly I saw a strange look come over his face. He was staring past me, down the ship, and it seemed as though he saw something incredible there. I followed his eyes, and saw one of the funniest, and at the same time one of the most pathetic things. It was a girl. She was nearly naked, brown as Hawaiian girls are, and making weird gestures with her hand, her face, and her entire body. She was more on her stomach than on her knees, and it was plain that she was terribly afraid of something which we could not see.

Now in the first place there should not have been another woman besides myself on the ship, and certainly not an Hawaiian girl. Her presence was as much of a mystery as her actions. Captain Judd called out to her in English, not knowing her island language, but she only gesticulated more and more, and seemed to be even more frightened, cowering at the foot of the rope ladder that led up to us.

Suddenly, and before the Captain could get to his feet or go to investigate, there was a sharp cry behind her, and one of the Kanaka sailors who had appeared from nowhere sprang at her with a knife gleaming in his hand.

It was at this instant that the Captain gave a demonstration of real rapid thinking. The girl was quicker than her assailant, ducked under the ladder, and scurried across the deck to momentary safety. I screamed. But just as the sailor was in the act of springing at the terror-stricken child again, Captain Judd pulled his revolver from his pocket and fired into the air.

That was enough.

The Kanaka dropped the knife and stood there cowering. The girl held her ground, almost as much afraid as the man. We went down to investigate.

The matter was not really as serious as it seemed on the face of it. A little questioning from Mr. Coddy, who knew enough Hawaiian to justify his berth, revealed that the girl had become the "wife" of the sailor and had stowed away on the *Tropic Star* the night before we sailed, just in order not to be separated from him. Three days and three nights she had gone without food and water, hiding in a barrel, until she could not stand it any longer. Then she came out and looked for white people, in whom she had more confidence than in those of her race, and because she was uncertain (apparently with reason) as to the reception her lover would give her.

Well, it turned out to be rather funny than otherwise. The Captain was all for punishing the girl and putting her in irons, but I saw no particular advantage in that, and I determined to take her on as a servant and finally got my way with the skipper. I made her promise that she would not try to join her Kanaka lover, but that she would take care of me during the journey. I must say that she kept her word.

I had Nakai, as I called her (her real name was something like that, or at least started with those sounds) for over six months. She learned English fairly well, too, and turned out to be very sweet and eager to please me. But one day she ran away with an American sailor in Pagopago Harbor, Samoa, and that was the last I knew of her.

CHAPTER X

The picture of the steam locomotive railway at Yokohama seaside, drawn by Utagawa Hiroshige III, 1874.

So much for my early cruising. My experiences in the Polynesian Islands, the Tahitian and Samoan group, are chiefly descriptive, and we will pass over them here in order to get more quickly into my life in the true Orient. My lonely voyaging ended, I could not long resist the beckoning of that spiritual finger, and, despite another marriage and other thwarting circumstances, I set out once more.

I think my true life began in Japan, and I almost wish it would end there. My honeymoon for a second cruise in the sea of matrimony with Harry Gillig, was really a double one, for I became equally the spouse and the mistress of an ancient and glorious spirit that reigns supreme over those sweet, civilized countries where even the least peasants are philosophers and where Man is closer to the elements of life.

When you think of Japan you must recognize the presence of a miracle. I do not pretend to know much about the history of that peach and poppy country, but every schoolgirl knows what Commodore Perry did in 1854, and everybody who reads the newspapers knows about the efficiency and progress of the Japan of today. From a state of feudalism to a modern civilization in less than one hundred years! That is the miracle, and a fairly good key to the agile mind of the Japanese race.

Before launching upon my putterings around in that country I am going to open a history book (knowing nothing very accurate by myself) and sketch a little picture of what happened there before I came, so that you can understand what had previously occurred and also what was then going on.

For centuries, it appears, there had been no real ruler in Japan. The military rule under the Shoguns or feudal lords had kept the race in a condition of beautiful out-of-touch-ness with the West and Western progress. Beautiful, but impractical. Then, in 1868, the Shogun rule was overthrown. The "Open Door" policy of Perry became a reality. One year later the first telegraph appeared. Two years more, and there were lighthouses and charted waters for ships. Still another year, and there were postage stamps, post offices and railways springing into existence. A university was built. A commission was sent to America and to Europe to study this thing called "modern progress." In 1873 the Christian calendar was adopted. In four years more a postal treaty with foreign nations was signed. Soon after came a constitution, a new penal code, and the gold standard for money was adopted.

And in 1899, the extra-territorial rights which had been granted to foreign nations there to protect their citizens against "barbaric laws" were abolished as being unnecessary. Japan, in that year, was recognized by the rest of the world as a civilized power, worthy of confidence from the Western point of view, and began to be taken note of as a possible clever rival in world affairs.

Only thirty years were needed to bring about a complete metamorphosis of principle and civilization. That was a miracle if ever one occurred.

Such are the wonderful Japanese.

Now when I first went to Japan these things were happening. Many had already happened. The land of poppies and cherries was bursting out of its cocoon.

But enough of history and schoolbooks. What fascinated me was the people. It has always been the people, the little native people of any country in the world, who have been interesting to me.

And it is strange, in a way, that the human beings of Borneo or Hottentot Land or China or Tibet are very much indeed like the human beings of Milwaukee or Beverly Hills. Believe it or not.

I sailed into the bay of Yokohama in April. Smells of spices reached me several miles before the lofty head of Fujiyama lifted up and nodded its welcome to me. I always think of that brilliant and mystery-covered mountain as an incarnation of Buddha, of Confucius, of all the entire East which the West can never understand. Kipling's rhyme on the subject is much more right than we know until we have been there to learn.

Spices and strange oriental smells greeted me, and the soul of Japan, like a little white bird, fluttered down and hid somewhere in my heart. Funny and picturesque little boats swarmed the waters. Little men, gleaming and naked, with poles or paddles, worked vigorously in them. Every kind of ship known to man, I guess, lay crowded along the docks or was pushing its way in or out of the harbor.

I had always read that Yokohama was a sort of fusing-pot for the world, and the truth of the threadbare old expression became clear to me on that day at the close of the 19th century.

Color, color, color. Greens and reds and beautiful dirty

shades and hues of every description fluttered or moved about the shore-line as we were warped in. I was sorry that I had left my schooner in Samoa. It would have been magnificent to have formed part of that tapestry. But the sounds, new sounds of new voices, rose above the steamer's mechanical noises. New birds, new kinds of gulls and other seabirds, soared or flapped over the ship and the docks ahead. Everything was pungently Eastern, pungently Japanese.

And, as though a magician had produced it out of his kimono sleeve or out of a little box with a wooden wand, there lay the Bund of Yokohama, bristling and stretched out for me to walk on and to play with and to love.

Imagine an immigration pier in Oriental Japan! It was real, nevertheless, and the quiet, firm professional manner of the officials, excessively polite and speaking English so over-perfectly as to be funny, was one of the preliminary shocks of my journey. But these new-civilized little men handled us in a way which could give pointers to the present-day gentlemen of Ellis Island. If this be treason, let us profit by it.

Yokohama! 'Rikishas, scuffling of padded feet. Swishing of kimonos. Scurrying of little boys. Cries and calls and barks of 'rikisha boys and the calls of the blind shampooers. Distinctly Oriental. The world and the sun had shifted and I was in the land I had dreamed about.

We went to a hotel. It was supposedly English, but the supposition ended there, for the owner and entire personnel were native, and a quaint structure it was too. However, there was real courtesy, forced but perfected. The Japanese are, as everybody knows, the most polite people in the world and the most perfectly poised. There was also comfort such as Europeans desire, although the Japanese themselves do not sleep in a bed but are willing to supply such "silly devices" to the barbaric Westerners who come to visit them.

But when I desired a bath I got my first glimpse of the unsettled state of fusion between the West and the East that was going on.

The bath existed all right. It consisted of a little wooden box right next to the stove that heated the water. It was all in readiness for me and I was pleased at the prospect. However I found no soap, and upon inquiry, I learned that it was considered the height of discourtesy to utilize the cake I had brought with me, because the tradition was that soap in the water would make it dirty and unpleasant for the next person. I will not emphasize the itchy and questionable feeling that my first bath there gave me when I realized that I was not the first to use that tubful.

How can I describe the country without being wordy and wearily descriptive? The sheer pleasure of being pulled about in a 'rikisha, or *kuruma*, as the natives called them, was more than a novelty: it was a voluptuous, personal thrill. The runners, or *Kurumaya*, powerful little men in short blue cotton tights and shirts, their straw sandals and huge mushroom hats, are high in the list of picturesque things in Japan. And this brings me abruptly to a story which, while it is not my own, concerns some one I knew very well.

Her name we will conceal under the similar one of Daphne Stebbins. She came from Bellows Falls, Vermont. She had come on the same steamer as my husband and I. She was very good-looking and about 35 years old. She was eminently virginal and she suffered from it. I say suffered, although it is very doubtful if she knew either that she was suffering or from what.

Miss Stebbins came to Japan as a tutoress to two of the nastiest, most horribly spoiled little children I have ever had the misfortune to know. All during the trip from San Francisco they had made miserable the life of every person on the ship, and there was not a corner of any deck where one could find peace from their rowdiness and interference. Apparently they had never been subjected to discipline, and poor Miss Stebbins was having a fairly bad time of it.

The children, in fact, were the reason we got into conversation, and it was not long before both my husband and I liked Miss Stebbins immensely and were quite sorry for her. For she was really a romantic soul . . . an unusual thing for the typical New Englander of her origin and upbringing . . . and had taken the chance of escorting these two incorrigibles to the East to visit their family (a tea-merchant father and an ex-chorus-girl mother, I learned later) as a sort of escape from a life which was drying her and stifling her.

As we talked with her every day, I learned after a while that she had once had a sort of love affair with a young professor in Tufts, but that he had jilted her for some younger and wealthier Boston girl. She suffered terribly from the memory. It was all very banal, but the effect upon her was not to be denied. I shall be bold enough to say that Miss Stebbins was suffering from sexual starvation. It was evident from the way she acted with all the men on the ship . . . even with my husband . . . . Not that I cared. It was likewise probable that she had never known physical love and that its mysteries both offended and attracted her at the same time. Puritan training in constant struggle with the simple, strong human emotions and desires. In short, Miss Stebbins was a little bit mad, and the events which ensued are proof of it.

By the time we reached Yokohama my husband and I had become very good friends with her, and we prevailed upon her to bring her two little devils and to stop at our hotel until the parents should come down from Osaka, the father's Eastern headquarters, and claim them. She did, and she was very glad to have our company. So was I, for a woman sometimes needs the company of women.

The first signs of what was going to happen escaped me completely, for who would have imagined anything so startling from a Bellows Falls old maid? She sat beside me while our 'rikisha runner pulled us through the lovely city, chattering about this and that, and we both amused ourselves at the odd signs of the tradesmen in front of the shops of the foreign quarter. These were funny enough, by the way. One read: "Respectable ladies and gents invited to have fits" in front of an enterprising tailor shop. Another, an eager furrier, read: "Furs made from our skins or yours," and another, a barber's, stated brutally: "American and British gentlemen's heads cut."

Well, I did notice that Miss Stebbins grew more and more ill at ease in the 'rikisha. I remember remarking to her about the magnificent torso of our runner as he pattered along with our 260 or more pounds behind him, his muscles rippling under his yellow-tanned skin, his solid legs pulling tirelessly. I remember later also that she was a little tense in her reply to my remark, and that she mumbled something about his being handsome.

We drew up at the One Hundred Stairs of the famous Fujita tea-house where all the foreign colony of Yokohama daily has its rice-cakes and tea and conversation, and there we got down, preliminary to climbing up there. Miss Stebbins went up to our runner, and tried in pidgin English to tell him to wait for us.

She had scarcely uttered ten words, however, before she wavered, choked and collapsed right on the little man. Impassively, he took her elbows in his hands and held her there while I ran to her assistance. She had not fainted, but she seemed to be suffering from some sort of emotional shock. As I took her in my arms, she reached out wildly and seemed to be clawing at the chest of the little runner. The incident lasted only a matter of seconds, and an English gentleman, getting out of another 'rikisha, offered us his help. He practically carried the young woman up the long flight of stairs. A brandy and soda revived her a little, but she was still restless and seemed not inclined to talk, not even to explain, if she could, what had happened nor to be pleasant to the very nice Englishman who had carried her . . . no mean gallantry, either . . . up all those stairs.

Suddenly she excused herself, saying that she felt badly again, and that she wanted to get the air for a few moments. I remembered later that she did seem a little wild-eyed. At all events, I began to worry when she did not return after some twenty minutes, and I went to look for her. Not a sign.

Upon inquiry, I discovered that she had taken the 'rikisha and had gone off, leaving me to find another to return in. I took advantage of the Englishman's kind offer to see me back to the hotel, and I left Fujita without having enjoyed at all my first tea in the most curious tearoom in the world.

At the hotel, no sign of Miss Stebbins. No word. Nothing. She had disappeared. I told the story to my husband, who did not take it very seriously, but when dinner was over and she made no appearance he was as worried as I.

After dinner we went to the American consul and told the story, and the concern he showed told us that there was a certain danger. Not only that, but we had the two incorrigible children on our hands all night, for Miss Stebbins did not come back.

Inquiry on the part of the Yokohama police revealed that the 'rikisha runner who had taken her away from Fujita had not returned to his post, but that was absolutely all that could be learned, and the hotel was in a buzz of worried excitement.

Three days later the parents of the two children were due, and I was prepared to tell them a story which I thought pretty tragic. But that morning early, as I was dressing for town, there was a rapid knock on my door and Miss Stebbins appeared.

I scarcely recognized her at first. Not only because she was so bedraggled and drawn and changed-looking, but because there was a new light in her eyes, almost a new personality.

"Oh, my friend!" she kept saying, and clung to me, almost as though she were frightened. "Oh, my friend!"

Then it came out.

I was never so surprised in my life as when I heard her amazing story. The fact is that her imagination and her normal desires had been struggling against her Puritanical training, and finally, under the influence and freedom and trance of the East, she had succumbed. And in succumbing she had gone to an extreme that most people would have been squeamish about.

She had, in fact, fallen in love with the 'rikisha runner.

Perhaps "love" is not the word. It was a physical thing. She raved on about his strength, his quiet power, his calm, his manly simplicity. It was almost funny.

I gathered that she had taken the poor man by storm, and that her disappearance was "one of those things."

Well, the upshot of it was that I had to save her from scandal and from criticism. We concocted a story about her having been lost. I forget the details now, but it was a fairly good one and perfectly possible because things of that kind had happened before. I got her dressed decently again and made into a respectable-appearing woman once more, and we presented her at dinner in such a way that she became a sort of popular heroine. I imagine the American consul suspected something, but he was a good fellow, and did not ask too many embarrassing questions. As to the parents of the brats, they came, and were too smug to suspect anything out of the way.

Anyhow, they departed, all four of them, and I never heard of her again except to have a little note about three weeks afterwards, saying:

"Keep my secret, dear friend. The book is open."

I wonder what that meant, that last.

CHAPTER XI

Japanese acrobat performer Hayatake Torakichi.
Ukiyo-e by Utagawa Kuniyoshi, 1857.

So much for one set of influences exposed to the Orient. But my story is bigger than that, and while we are at it, let me tell a curious piece of history concerning the 100 steps and the Fujita tearoom which has nothing to do with Miss Stebbins and her troubles.

Anyone who has been to Japan will remember it, doubtless, but for those who have never been able to get away from Main Street or Broadway (are they not much the same place after all?) here is a story which never could have happened anywhere except in the Orient.

There was once upon a time ... and not such a very long time ago either ... (about 1881) ... a Japanese acrobat. Now an acrobat in Japan is, shall we say, of a different mentality from those we see in American vaudevilles and continental music-halls. This was a man not only intelligent but also religious, and his art ... he called it so ... was inspired by Buddha.

After many years of public display and glory, when he was getting to be an old man, he decided to perform his greatest and most dangerous feat. This was to ride on horseback up the 100 stairs leading to Fujita with his little daughter standing on his shoulders, and then to come down again (alone this time) standing on his head, holding the reins with his feet.

He did just this, while a great crowd applauded, and he consecrated his "stunt" to the praise of Buddha.

But this was not enough. He decided then that his art could only express his gratitude to Buddha by riding up and down all the long stairs in Japan and performing the same acrobatic feat ... and there are many high places with stairs leading to them in the country.

For one year the acrobat continued his strange performance, a sort of vow of gratitude and recognition, until one day, having returned to Yokohama, he again mounted the 100 steps of Fujita and came down, with his legs waving in the air.

But it appears that on the night before he had committed the sin of stealing (only for a short time, mind you) the wife of a fellow circus rider, and so the Great Buddha willed it that he should be punished. At the forty-third step his horse stumbled and down he came, breaking his neck, and landing at the bottom definitely dead. The rival acrobat completed the punishment by stealing the daughter of the dead man, and everything was all right, naturally.

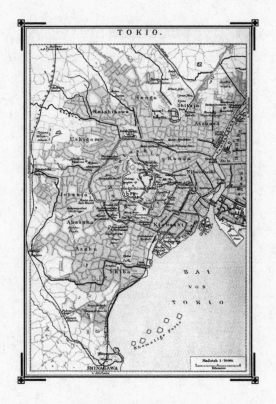

TOKIO.

BAI VON TOKIO

Ehemalige Forts

SHINAGAWA

CHAPTER XII

Map of Tokyo, 1896. Brockhaus Encyclopedia.

ut to return to my own adventures. One thing I recall about my first trip to Japan is most amusing. About a month after the departure of Miss Stebbins, my husband and I started on a sort of tour in the country. I say tour; perhaps it would be more correct to say journey of exploration, for actually we rumbled off in a sort of cart drawn by oxen, piled high with our baggage, and incidentally containing my very uncomfortable spouse and my equally uncomfortable self.

Our direction, in general, was Kyoto, although we never got there, for reasons which will appear later. Actually we got about thirty miles away from Yokohama in some three days, stopping at little paper or bamboo places as substitutes for hotels and having rather a time of it.

Our way led more or less over high rugged hills, and for that reason we had been advised to take the ox-cart. Of that, no matter. On the third day my husband and I were pretty tired and decided to rest from the bouncing and jouncing of the journey. We accomplished this in another paper-walled house in a town whose name I do not remember. I do recall that I slept for several hours, in spite of the fact that the only bed I had in this primitive "hotel" was the floor, a mat and a little wooden rest for my head. (The Japanese women use this sort of thing to preserve their very complicated head-dress.) On the second day, my husband went out, rather stiffly and sorely, but with a lot more courage than I had. I remained "in bed" and cursed the day I had taken the ox-cart.

I recall that I heard some sort of disturbance ... voices or something ... next door, but paid little attention to it. Suddenly and without warning there was a great crash and the body of a man came through the paper wall ... right on top of me.

It was an Englishman. And strangely enough it was the very Englishman who had carried my friend Daphne Stebbins up the long stairs on the day of her great adventure.

He was embarrassed, to say the least.

Imagine being in a drowse and having a strange man come hurtling through the wall on top of you! But it was so funny ... or so I thought ... that I did nothing but laugh, while he babbled apologies. These were accepted with laughter, and my Englishman and I had a long conversation, quite unmindful of the buzzing of the Japanese proprietor who was lamenting his broken partition.

On top of all this my husband came in and there was more embarrassment because he could not see the joke. In fact all he could see was the Englishman ... a rather fine-looking fellow ... sitting there smoking a cigarette on the floor while I was in my boudoir and clad in little else than a kimono.

Well, it was all very absurd. Huntingdon-Meer, as the Englishman was called, was pitifully embarrassed. Why are British persons of a certain class always so embarrassed and pink? And my husband was very angry and gruff to him. He went away, naturally, and moved into another room where the wall was still undamaged, and left me to face my irate spouse alone.

Then began something which was really unfortunate. I wish the male of my species had more sense of humor, for my husband was vaguely under the impression that I had planned all this, and that the paper wall's breaking was merely part of an immense flirtation.

Net result: I *did* have a flirtation with my wall-crashing acquaintance, and a lot of fun it was too.

But that is the other part of this story.

You will gather, if you have not already done so, that all my life I believed in what are cheaply called "flirtations." Our good friend Mrs. Grundy will insist that they are immoral, impolite, cheap, etc., etc., etc., etc. Especially so for married women or married men.

But let me explain my idea, boldly and frankly, and I am willing to stand for anybody's opinion after that.

In the first place flirtation is only a word, a name, for something which is not only amusing but instructive. There is no fact more fundamental than this: the basic relationship between male and female (whether human or animal) is that of pursuit and evasion. Not only biology and history prove it, but common observation. Now the human animal has the advantage over other animals (if indeed it is an advantage) in that he has a reasoning, imaginative mind. So this pursuit really becomes something much more than sex-pursuit. There is still that, of course, but it is enlarged and developed into a much more amusing game in proportion as the humans who engage in it are gifted with reason, imagination, intuition, and so forth.

Flirtation, as I mean it, is or can be the most fascinating pastime in the world. It can employ more wit than political intrigue, more imagination than writing novels, more comprehension of your fellow humans than applied psychology, and more intuition than gambling in Wall Street. If your opponent in the game is clever and your equal or superior at this sort of fencing, there is nothing more thrilling. If not, there is no better way to discover a bore and discard him than to flirt a little.

A friend of mine once expressed it pretty well. "You push Button A, and Thing A happens. Then you push Buttons B, C, D, and so on. If it all works out according to formula, you have discovered just another uninteresting person. But if, when you push Button D, something happens that you've not bargained for . . . then you get interested."

Well, that's the way I feel about flirting.

It does not always end in love, nor in bed, nor in any of the conventional story-book ways. Thank God. Sometimes it gives you a real friend whom you respect. Sometimes it just peters out after you've had your fun. Sometimes it gets you into trouble. You never know. That, of course, is part of the thrill.

But to go back to my Englishman who fell through the wall. I have never been overly drawn to Englishmen. Nor to Americans nor to any of the Nordic races, for that matter. Perhaps my prejudice, if it is one, came from some early experience.

Anyhow, here's the story.

Huntingdon-Meer was the India-Service type of Oxonian. (Perhaps he was Cambridge, or some other University, but he was the *type* I mean.) He was tall, well-made, strong-minded, traveled, and knew his Orient like a book. After he had gotten over his shocked embarrassment at discovering I had a husband (they all get over husbands, given half a chance) he really interested me with his stories about India. I tried to get my husband interested too, but . . . well I was young enough to believe it could be done. I tried to explain to my spouse, too, that flirtation had absolutely no bearing on my regard and love for him. Well, women who will read this will realize how silly that was. And when Huntingdon-Meer finally broke down, flushing and stammering and eager and boyish, and told me that he had followed us all the way from Yokohama and had crashed the wall on purpose, just to get to know me ... well, that settled it. I played the princess, and he was my very overgrown, very eager page.

Naturally, to keep peace with my husband our conversations were infrequent and more or less under cover. Then one day my husband wanted to go on with our exploration. I did not want to, not only because I was having fun with my page, but also because it was too uncomfortable. A breach was saved when my Englishman appeared with three horses ... pretty good ones, which he had procured mysteriously ... and proposed that we all three go on together on horseback, sending the baggage along in the ox-cart.

The idea won out, and off we set, albeit my husband was not very enthusiastic and in fact rather gruff about it. It did not last long, however, for an accident happened.

His horse shied at something imaginary, tripped, stumbled, and fell with him, and we had to take him, pretty badly shaken but not seriously hurt, back to the hotel. There we all decided to return to Yokohama.

We did, and there things began to happen.

In the first place, a telegram awaited my husband at the American consulate, calling him hurriedly to San Francisco. It was not a matter of life and death, but one of comfort or poverty, which, in its way, is just as or more important. A matter of business.

Off he went for two months. There was nothing else for him to do but to go. And it was better all round that I should stay behind.

I stayed, although at the last minute I did not want to and later circumstances proved that I was correct in my intuition.

Right then and there began what I like to call my "English Episode in Japan." An unkind person might call it something less euphemistic, but it seems that my word is as good as any.

Huntingdon-Meer (not his right name, of course, but a convenient and "near" substitute) projected himself violently into my life as soon as my husband departed. He began by protesting his platonic affection for me, and he ended by stammering about this thing he called "love." We played about the city (which he knew intimately), but he made the tactical error of presenting me to Baron Takamini, and that ruined everything.

Takamini was a man, a real one. Small, as are most Japanese, he was none the less the most perfect specimen of man I have ever seen. He was immensely rich (not that it mattered), politically and socially prominent, of old and noble family who were supposed to have descended from one of the last great Shoguns, and endowed with a singularly intense mind which had been developed at Yale, Heidelberg, and at the Sorbonne. He was a curious combination of Eastern and Western personality and culture. Furthermore, he was handsome as only an Oriental can be handsome.

I remember an old London popular song that ran "Never introduce your donah to a pal," and it dealt with precisely the same error as our friend Huntingdon-Meer made with me. The Baron liked me and I liked him, and the Englishman saw it and suffered. In fact he suffered so much that he complained to me about it, and immediately his cause was lost as far as I was concerned. I do not believe there is a woman alive, or ever has been, who can stand whimpering on the part of a full-grown man. Anyhow, I cannot. I was ashamed of my friend. Perhaps I had better express it "ashamed *for* him." Not only that, I told him so, and that ended it . . . or almost.

The "almost" comes in when, one night, he came rushing to my hotel and made a scene. Talk about your Anglo-Saxon self-control and so-called phlegmatism. It is all right as far as it goes, but when it breaks down there remains a rather pathetic spectacle. I was dining with the Baron in my rooms. My former flirt came up, unannounced, broke into my suite without waiting for my servant, and acted as if he had been my husband, or something.

I will never forget the contrast between the little, poised man of the East who sat there contemplating his friend, smoking a cigarette, and the tall blond-headed, sunburned India-Service man, broken with self-pity.

I told him he had no right, no claim to me. I tried to show him that flirtation was a pastime, a device for amusing two intelligent persons and for studying one another. But he had taken it too seriously.

He became violent. He bellowed and roared at me. He even called me names which were scarcely consistent with the code of a gentleman. It was pretty bad.

Then something happened.

The Baron got to his feet, not hurriedly, not in a rage. He stepped over to Huntingdon-Meer, and in the twinkling of an eye that big body was on the floor . . . almost without any noise . . . and not only silent but completely paralyzed.

Then the Baron rang for the servant, said that his friend had

had a stroke or something similar, took every care that he was properly treated and carried down to a 'rikisha and sent home to his own apartments with an attendant.

"He will be well again in perhaps half an hour," he told me. "It is too very bad."

The next day I heard that my Englishman had sailed for Bombay, and that was that.

Baron Takamini showed me Japan. He revealed the East to me as no one else could have done. He initiated me into the strange cosmopolis that is Yokohama. Its different racial settlements, its dives, its secret places, the sad and curious places along the Bund where sailors of all nations try so hard to amuse themselves.

But best of all he took me into the most remarkable capital in the world . . . Tokio . . . and made me understand his people.

A thing that struck me, and that I remember even to this very late day in my life, was the process of fusion. Not only the assimilation of European life and thought and methods by the Japanese, but the change that comes over Europeans and Americans who live long enough in that country. There is one story which illustrates this latter point, and I think it is worth telling.

It concerns a woman. She was the wife of an American exporter, a man much too old for her, but rather a fine fellow in his way. She had grown into the social life of Tokio – as one so easily does – and her routine became one of dinners, official and private, and gatherings more or less formal.

Personally, I had enough of that sort of thing in my first month in the capital and got away from it as soon as I could.

Mrs. Blakelock was getting towards forty. She had been a very beautiful girl, and she retained her charm physically in a surprising manner. But her mind had become affected by the constant social demands upon her. Furthermore, her husband, a man of affairs whose entire life was consecrated to the advancement of his company's business, seemed so occupied that he paid rather less attention to her than a woman likes to receive.

Result: she had a lover.

The lover was a youngish American college boy who had "gone wrong," as they expressed it in the colony there. Actually, he had come over to Japan with the export department of a large American firm, had let the life there go to his head, had started drinking "seriously," had lost his job, and had found . . . a "meal ticket." In our modern times the French word "gigolo" would have found a fair application.

Larry Meaker had been born for the movies. He would have been a perfect running mate for our "Great lovers of the Silver Sheet," but there being no silver sheet in those days, he had no natural profession open to him. His face was a little too perfect, his mustache had been trained to droop with the correct Adolph Menjou manner. He was witty, sophisticated, poised and pleasing. He danced well . . . too well.

In short, Larry Meaker, when first I met him, was the sort of young man for whom all the Mrs. Blakelocks in the world unavoidably fall, and this Mrs. Blakelock did so, as naturally and naïvely as you please. And he did very nicely, dressed well to attract her, prospered and drank himself into a sort of social position, despised by all the men, loved by his mistress, and afforded her the pleasure of being envied by other dowagers who had not been able to make such a "find."

But the husband was no fool.

A solid, stolid man, trying his best to sell more electrical machinery (or whatever it was he was selling) to the Japanese government than they could use, he failed to notice the liaison for over two years. Then one day, moved by one of those bursts of sentimental feeling that overcome the T.B.M.'s occasionally, he came home unexpectedly to give the "little woman" a pleasant surprise.

He surprised her, all right. He surprised her in the arms of Larry Meaker, and it broke in him that little catch which separates madness and sanity in all of us. Momentarily insane, he rushed to his study, took out a tremendous old revolver he had carried somewhere in Wyoming years before, and emptied it into the well-tailored body of his wife's paid lover.

Such stories are not nice, but this one has a moral.

The moral came out when, three days after her husband had been apprehended and her lover cremated according to Japanese custom, she appeared at a well-known bar in Tokio and said, with real feeling:

"Isn't it horrible? Now I can't go to the Embassy dinner."

But to return to my Baron.

The first thing he did was to get me away from Tokio's foreign colony. He rented a house for me in a suburb, and I must confess that there never was such a quaint, curious, and splendid house in the world.

It had ten rooms and was built of bamboo and paper, and I had a bedroom . . . something I had always wanted . . . furnished completely in red lacquer. I had thirty servants, all trained and uniformed, and I began the life of a real Japanese aristocrat . . . rather more emancipated than any Japanese woman, but quite distinct from life in the foreign colony.

And there the East poured in on me and filled my very marrow with its mysteries, its secrets, its old-world, oddly civilized way of thinking. My husband was not to return until several months later than he had planned, and I had an opportunity to study this beautiful, pink, hardy, human country of Japan such as is given to few Westerners.

I think what fascinated me most about the Japanese was their religious side, and their "bushido," or knightly code, an almost poetic thing which calls to mind the days of knight-errantry, and King Arthur and his Round-Table knights. "Bushido" is the soul of Japan. It is the root of their far-famed politeness, their courtesy, their admirable self-control, their poise.

But under it all is the deep religious fervor of the race. Christian missionaries have accused them of superficiality and sham, but Christian missionaries are wrong. Buddhists, Confucians, Shintoists, and even Christians, there is a richness of feeling and a reality of emotion in their worship of whatever-it-may-be that I, at least, have never seen equaled among peoples of the West, save, perhaps, among those called "uncivilized."

Buddhism and Confucianism I need not comment upon. But some idea of Shinto is worthy of mention.

In this philosophy, the world of the living is governed by the dead. The dead become gods, and every impulse, every act, every thought of man during life is the work of a god. It is, moreover, a simple code. It is scarcely a religion at all. It is partly a political conception. It runs under the Japanese thought, whatever other religious creeds the people profess. Its architecture is simple, cold, unornate. Its ceremonies are moderate and dry. And, because of it, the bodies of the Japanese are not buried, but cremated, in order that the souls which pass on may be unhampered by the clay of life.

There were only 127,076 Shinto shrines in Japan in my day.

There were also 71,730 temples to Buddha and 180,129 priests consecrated to the worship of that benign deity.

It is worth thinking about.

Another curious thing . . . a thing completely misunderstood by the well-meaning missionaries from America and Europe . . . is the intertwining of religious ceremony with the so-called "vice" of the country.

Vice!

My Baron once took me to the formal opening of one of the houses of vice. It was conducted seriously, like the laying of a corner stone in an American city, but with a religious ceremony as an incorporated part of it.

I wonder if this is really as shocking as the missionaries would have us believe? What I observed about vice in Japan is that it is not vicious. By that I mean that the government not only tolerates institutions of this sort, but finances them and licenses them. The girls who "work" in such places are often well-educated and are, except in the low dives run for and by foreigners along the water fronts, seldom conscious of anything very wrong with their profession.

There is an underlying idea which is fundamental. The fact of sex is a perfectly well accepted one in Japan. The sex act is known to be perfectly natural and normal. Prostitution is a profession which antedates any other in the world, for the reason that, like all true trades, there is a real need for it. There is little or no repression in Japan. Prostitution fills a want, and is therefore considered quite in order. The Japanese do not sentimentalize about these things. Their sophistication is as real as it is unconscious.

Then there is another side to the question. The women.

A typical case came to my attention in Tokio. An elegant Japanese gentleman squandered his fortune in trying to become even more elegant. He made debts, and in his country debts are a matter of honor.

Now the gentleman had two very beautiful daughters who were flowers of rare good breeding and high culture. The father, confronted with debts of honor which he could not pay, delicately carved himself across the stomach in the noble gesture of Hari-kiri, leaving the girls, and a nice, but useless, widow. The family honor was at stake. And the next thing that the two girls did was to apply for a job in one of the government-owned houses of prostitution. They paid the debt, and later married fine young men of some of the best families. Where is the wrong? The Japanese place a stress on virtue, but not upon the man-made symbols of that elusive quality.

But that is something which every person must figure out for himself, I suppose.

Speaking of this vague thing called virtue, I have two stories, both conflicting, to tell. One concerns my Baron, and the other some one whom I scarcely even knew. If you, reader, are one who seeks a moral in stories, you can supply it. I will not attempt to do so.

Things continued very much as described between Baron Takamini and myself. There was no monotony. There were pleasure and observation and a keen sense, on my part at least, that I could learn from him a little about the extraordinary race to which he belonged.

Himself, he seemed amused at me, especially at the things I considered wonderful in his own race and country. I suppose I appeared naïve to him, and doubtless I was.

But a shadow appeared upon our horizon.

Perhaps "shadow" is not the exact word. Perhaps, for him, it was sunshine. But it appeared.

Its name was Marcia Penelope Darnley, only nobody called her that. In the English-speaking colony of Tokio she was called Penn Darnley, and she was the daughter of the Reverend Carlton Darnley, one-time director of English instruction in one of the important schools controlled by the American missions in Japan. They both hailed from some small town in Wisconsin . . . I have forgotten which one . . . and had been only a short time in the country.

Penn met Baron Takamini and me at the Embassy ball . . . the one that Mrs. Blakelock was unable to attend, by the way. She was a very pretty girl. She was blonde. She was tall. She had fine, clean features, and the most beautiful hands I have ever seen on any woman. Also she had a careful education of the academic type and was very much better informed on most subjects than the average girl.

And with her blond hair she had black eyes.

My Baron was presented to her by Charlie Furst of the Consulate. The Baron did not wait a moment before bringing her to me . . . he was a gentleman to his fingertips . . . and I saw immediately that he was more than a little drawn to her.

Penn Darnley's attitude towards Baron Takamini was not what one could call condescending, yet it smacked at first of that. It was really one of great dignity, mixed with just a little fear. But she too was "interested."

We had a triangular conversation which was not perfectly at ease. We missed dances, and then Charlie Furst took me off while the Baron glided away with her in his perfect European waltz-meter, laughing and looking brighter than I had ever seen him.

I must confess that there was a slight tinge of jealousy in my voice later on, when I said to him:

"And what do you think of the new American generation?"

He answered simply: "She is like a flower."

I was not too pleased.

Next day the Baron was late at my house. He was entirely honest about the fact that he had seen Miss Darnley, had taken her over the same ground of exploration where he and I had begun, had been presented to her father, had accepted invitations for future dinners and teas and croquet (golf had not yet made its appearance in the East) and every other kind of familiar reunion.

He was not boastful in telling me. Had he been, I would not probably have cared so much. He was rather wistful. He seemed boyish, and I had never seen him like that. I was piqued. My vanity was hurt. After all, she was "only a little Wisconsin girl." She knew nothing of life, while I was a woman of the world.

Well, you know how we all are.

This grew. I made a scene one day. The Baron turned his long eyes upon me, perfectly expressionless, and told me straight out that he loved her. He was honest, Takamini.

Then I was ashamed. I did not and could not love the Baron, but I was very fond of him. And, woman-like, or even mother-like, I had a premonition that Penn Darnley could not and would not love him either. It was a curious interest on her part. Also on her father's part.

Things moved swiftly. One day my Baron came to me very humbly. He said he had a confession to make.

"It is about Miss Darnley," he said.

"What is it?"

"I am going to take her away. I am going to take her with me . . . somewhere. She must go away with me."

In a way, I was surprised.

"Have you mentioned it to her?" I asked him, rather cruelly.

"No. Tonight I will ask her. She will go."

I wish I had known then, had realized exactly, what he was going to ask her.

That night the Baron came to my house late, very late. One of my servants announced him. I was in bed and had to put on the inevitable kimono to receive him. I do not even remember if the servant was alarmed, but it seems likely that he would have been.

Takamini looked like death. There was a red welt across his face. His features were composed, as always, but there was a look in his eye that suggested madness.

"I have come to wish you good-by."

"Good-by. Then she will go?" I asked foolishly.

I should have known.

"No, my friend." It was as though a marble statue were speaking. "No, she will not go. But I go."

I remember that I made some feeble remark, and that he kissed my hand stiffly, and then that he was gone.

Next morning, very early, I had another visitor. It was Penn Darnley.

She came in very stiffly also. There had never been much love lost between us. She brought her great mastiff Greedy with her on a leash, and she had a dog-whip in her hand.

"I suppose he came here and told you about it," she said.

I told her that I knew nothing, and then she went over a scene that made me ashamed of being an American. That Baron had told her plainly that he loved her, but that he could not marry her on account of family and religious traditions. He proposed that they should go away together, nevertheless . . . off into the dreamland of poppies . . . and live in love and bliss (and incidentally his great wealth) and flaunt the conventions.

Well, the effect was startling.

Penn Darnley, the little prude, had seen only something that she thought was "dirty." The man was asking her to become his mistress. Merely that. It was an insult to all our American girlhood. Our American girlhood is taught that it never becomes a mistress.

And little Miss Prude had been so conscious, too, that she was Anglo-Saxon, and a free member of a *White* race, and belonged to the Methodist-Episcopal Church. And the Baron Takamini, however "interesting," however "picturesque," was of another race. Thus the insult was doubled and magnified.

"Can you imagine!" she said to me, breathless and furious all over again. "Why, he asked me to live with him . . . me, a white woman!"

"Did he?" said I, able to think of nothing better.

"He did, the pig. Oh, my father warned me against them. I should have known better than to have trusted a Jap. They're always treacherous. They're always so polite . . . on the surface. But this one learned his lesson. He'll bother no more American girls. I whipped him, the dirty swine. I struck him across the face with this very whip, and if he were here I'd do it again."

Yes, and she would have set her dog on him, too.

She was graphic in telling the story. He had taken her hand

and kissed it. He had told her of the lovely flowered country of Japan where poets' dreams come true, and he had asked her to live with him near Nikko, the most beautiful city in the world, and to love him and to let him love her.

And she had blazed out at him:

"You dirty yellow man . . . !"

I wonder what she felt when she learned that Baron Takamini returned directly to his home after saying good-by to me, had bathed and perfumed his body, had brought his trusted servants round him, had taken a short sword encased in an ivory scabbard and beautifully engraved, and had cut himself open, returning to his glorious ancestors and becoming a Shinto god, then and there, to inspire the Japanese to hate more and more these blond foreigners who were insinuating themselves and their hateful creeds into this beautiful Land of Poppies.

I lost a friend. One of the best, one of the kindest, one of the most glorious men I have ever known.

"Dirty yellow man . . . !"

Mrs. Grundy, there's one for you.

CHAPTER XIII

Ships off the coast of Nagasaki in Japan, *c.* 1860s.

B
ut I promised you another story about "virtue."

This one brings me to Nagasaki, the Beach of the World. Time counts for little in a hit-or-miss book like this. I went there years after the things I have been talking about, but it applies right here in the story.

There was an American in Nagasaki who had fallen from grace. By that I mean that he had lost his birthright of manliness – had, according to the Grundy standard, "gone soft."

His name was Brandon. I suppose that it was not the correct one, but no matter. He was technically known as a beach-comber. That means a sort of groveling, spineless man who has lost his grip and who lives upon gratuities and leavings of the beach crowd. Furthermore, he was a drunkard. And doubly furthermore, he had "gone native," which means that he had a Japanese girl that he lived with ... if you can call it living.

Brandon was a sort of land-mark.

They pointed him out to you as a horrible example of what can happen to a fine, clean-cut man when the East "gets" him. He had been a port officer for one of the shipping companies and had lost his job through drink. That, at least, was the story.

As a matter of fact, I discovered later that he had lost his job because of his relations, quite public, they were, with the Japanese girl, and that he had taken to drink through losing it.

Be that as it may.

One day the whole colony was excited over news that spread from somewhere . . . as news will. Brandon had appeared at one of the good hotels for foreigners, well dressed, well groomed, clean and sober. He had a certain poise. He had money. He "affected," so they expressed it, a superior air. He dined, and made arrangements for a passage back to America. He paid for it in full and in cash.

And how the speculative tongues wagged.

Brandon left, and it was some weeks before the foreign colony learned that he had inherited valuable property and an estate from his grandfather. That seemed to be that.

"What a pity," said everyone. "How unfortunate that it had to go to such a weakling, such a tramp."

I had the good fortune to meet and to talk with the "girl he left behind him." She was a pretty thing, like a doll. She spoke very plausible English, and she was not at all unhappy at his departure. I asked her if she did not care.

"Honorable Mistress," she said, "know that there is no departure. He has not gone. Only his body has been removed."

Curious, this reply. I asked her what she meant, and I learned something more curious still.

She understood precisely what it meant that he should return to the land of his people when the head of his tribe should cease to exist. She understood that it was his duty to go away. But she was equally sure that only an earthly part of him had gone, but that his soul remained with her. And, Eastern, she had placed a charm over his body which should keep him from harm and bring him safe back to her.

It did.

And they bought a little house with one of those far-famed Japanese gardens where flowers are less in evidence than mossy stones, rivulet and curved red bridges, and they lived there happily ever afterwards, as the story book says.

And of course the colony was anxious to please, now that he had wealth, and a good name, and sartorial elegance. But he drank just as much, and enjoyed it, and no marriage ceremony was ever performed over him and his "wife," and . . . it is amusing, they were never "at home" to visitors.

Thus the beachcomber.

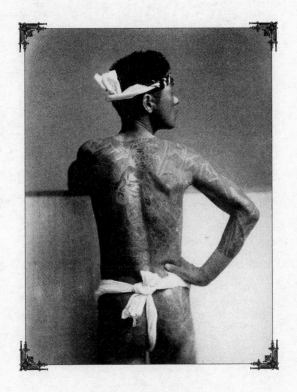

CHAPTER XIV

1585 Tattoo by S. Ogawa, *c.* 1890s.

I wish I could write fiction. I ought to be able to, because there has been such a succession of characters moving across the screen of my life. But I am too old to try now, and it is useless for me to attempt to do more with these characters than to tell about them as I saw them and to show what they meant to me.

While we are in Japan, there is Hori Tchio. Anybody who looked for the odd or the exotic in life would have been thoroughly satisfied with Hori Tchio.

He was an artist by profession and a gambler by preference, and a rather remarkable fellow in every way. To look at him, you would believe that he had stepped out of a gaudy melodrama during the intermission and had just neglected to remove his make-up and change his costume.

Hori Tchio went in for color and luxury in his clothes in a way that is not much in the nature of the Japanese ... rather more like the Chinese. I am not sure that Hori did not have some Chinese blood, as a matter of fact. His kimonos were of gorgeous, blazing silk, embroidered with symbolic designs or pastoral scenes. In fact, anything that was surprising or unusual could be looked for in the costumes of Hori Tchio.

And even more in the man himself.

Hori did a great service to both Japanese and foreigners.

He tattooed them. Now, this does not mean the cheap anchor and flowers and ladies' heads that you see on the arms and shoulders of sailors. Not Hori. He was an artist of the first water and his designs were really magnificent. He did tricks with them, too. For instance a design could be so arranged that it represented one thing when your muscles and skin were relaxed, and a totally different idea when they were flexed and tightened. It could be very surprising and effective.

An amusing story about Hori occurred in this way. There was a French attaché who was uxorious to a degree. His wife was young and beautiful and had him under a spell that was charming to see and also a little pathetic.

M. Rivaudin (if I recall his name correctly) brought his charming little spouse to Hori Tchio for a portrait. The great artist received them in this manner. There was tea. There were many servants who responded to a clapping of hands. There were heavy hanging curtains and rich tapestries and prints. Hori took his tablets and his brushes and studied the beauty of the lovely Western woman and translated it into paint. Many studies he made, and much conversation. Then he proposed an innocent game, the name of which I forget, but which is popular for gambling in the East.

Madame Rivaudin withdrew, pleading household duties, and went away in one of Hori's own beautifully decorated 'rikishas.

Monsieur Rivaudin played with Hori and was entranced with the man's brilliant conversation, his mellow wit and philosophy, his courtly manners.

Incidentally, he lost about £100 ... on credit, naturally, since everything is done on credit in Japan.

But the crux of the story is that after a certain amount of

saki and a certain number of hours with the curious artist, he was so impressed by the likenesses of his wife done by that master hand, that he decided to have one of them reproduced by tattooing on his person.

An appointment was made. Hori Tchio was not a slap-dash worker. His art was his mistress. And the job to be done was the height of his art. Therefore it would take about six months of careful work to reproduce Madame's beautiful features, life size, in a manner such that not one line, not one ray of her sunshine should be lost ... (he was not noted for modesty, this Hori Tchio) ... even the work of God might be made more splendid by the hand of Hori.

So it was arranged.

For three months Rivaudin went to his not unpainful sittings. The beautiful features of Madame grew and were glorified. But one fatal day came when he discovered that his charming and innocent wife had been deceiving him with Hori Tchio, artist and philosopher, ever since the day he had brought her there for her portrait.

It was a predicament.

The face was half done. His wife was lost to him. To efface the tattooing was not only painful, but would mean, under his contract with Hori, that he would be out not only the half but the full sum for the great artist's work. To carry on and have the work completed would take three months more. He would suffer the indignity of allowing the man who had stolen his love to decorate his person with the image of her who had destroyed his faith in humans. And all his life he would carry about with him the haunting and ironical features of this false lady.

You can imagine the story this made at the men's clubs. The solution, if one can call it that, was even more absurd and more like Hori Tchio.

Raging, our Frenchman went to the great Artist and Lothario. Calmly and philosophically he was received. There was a brief moment of storm . . . on Rivaudin's part, naturally. But the calm and poise of the oriental, subtle and magnificent in his self-control, carried the day.

Hori proposed the following plan.

Rivaudin owed him $500 (Mexican) for work already accomplished. Likewise he owed him $500 (Mexican) for work contracted for. And he was now suggesting that he should cheat the Great Artist not only by refusing payment but also demanding that the work of his hand be destroyed, removed, therefore lost to posterity. Hori was injured, really wounded in his pride.

But Hori was always generous, always sporting, always magnificent.

It was true that, through her weakness and his natural charm which no woman could resist, the Western wife of the Honorable Rivaudin had permitted him certain indulgences. It was also true that according to the absurd code of Europeans, Rivaudin was entitled to feel himself injured by such a trifling circumstance.

So they would bargain. They would make a sporting bargain, a true gambler's bargain. They would play. And the stakes would be the following: if the Honorable Rivaudin should win, he, Hori Tchio, would remove the magnificent work of art from the person of the unappreciative Westerner, and would release him from any payment . . . for what payment could atone for the destruction of a masterpiece? And he would engage to free the wife of the honorable Rivaudin from the spell of his Eastern charms so that she might return to her barbarian home where shoes are worn indoors.

But if he, Hori, should win – ah, that would be different!

Then the Honorable Rivaudin would pay him the entire sum of $1000 (Mexican) for the creation of a magnificent work of art upon his white-skinned person. He would permit that Hori Tchio, unequaled Artist, should complete the Masterpiece and earn the money which he had so fairly won. Furthermore, the Great Artist should retain his influence over the blond wife of the Westerner ... until such time as he grew tired of her – a time, perhaps, not far away ... but no matter. This was justice. This was fairness itself. This was even a concession.

And Monsieur Rivaudin agreed. And Monsieur Rivaudin lost.

CHAPTER XV

Photo of a Japanese courtesan by Felice Beato. *c.* 1890s.

But there is another story that is interesting, and a bit more personal. It concerns me and my husband, who returned to Japan as planned, after he had arranged his business.

The story is about the Geisha girls, a subject which can scarcely be missing from this or any other book on Japan.

In the first place let me say right here that the popular conception of Geisha girls is a wrong one. They are not in any way to be confused with prostitutes. Quite the contrary.

There were nearly two thousand Geisha houses in Japan when I was there. Here lived the girls, beautiful, doll-like creatures. They were professionally trained dancers, perfectly chaperoned, perfectly protected, perfectly educated. Their business was dancing: just that.

Like the Russian Ballet of the *ancien régime*, the girls were trained from babyhood almost, and became as nearly perfect in their art as it is possible for human beings to become. Japan was and is proud of them. Japan protects them and trains them and educates them. And if you are giving a reception you may employ them ... at a rather high cost ... to furnish part of the entertainment. Also you can go to their houses and spend an afternoon of high artistic value.

And when I see in the newspapers that a troupe of Geisha girls were excluded from a ship's entertainment on one of those round-the-world cruises . . . because they were supposed to detract from the moral tone . . . it makes me furious.

But to my story.

When my husband arrived he came with some men who were typical American business men "away from home" and on a spree. I overheard them proposing to secure the most famous Geisha house in Tokio for the night, and I understood that they had a wrong conception of what those little girls were. I was anxious to save them from a scandal, but I knew better than to show them how I felt, for they were rather merry after a day at the Club and plenty of whisky.

But I formed a plan.

Enlisting my hotel proprietor, a nice German fellow, my Japanese "courier," who was a sweet, active and methodical little woman, and a few friends whom I knew well enough to explain to, I formed a caravan of 'rikishas and went to the Geisha house before Friend Husband and his company got there, and made on the spot the arrangements necessary to hire it for the night.

It was not long before the stag party came and presented themselves at the door. They likewise had a courier . . . a man . . . who endeavored to rent the place. No avail. The old gentleman in gray kimono and pointed cap who was a sort of director (whatever his real title is I have no idea) politely but firmly told them that the place had already been taken. He was positive. No, the money made no difference. He was very sorry. No, not even for twice that sum, not for ten times. It was very sad, but it was so.

And we hid on the balcony and watched the chagrin of my husband and his party, who, slightly aflame with good Scottish liquid, went away again to some other place of amusement, leaving the fragrant Japanese air behind them rather blue with language which was not what the *"Jeune Fille"* should hear.

CHAPTER XVI

The Clipper *Grassendale* at Sea, Hong Kong School, 19th century.

And so I could go on, almost endlessly I feel, with the little personal notes, the anecdotes, the tiny-but-curious little experiences and stories. But when I have so much to tell, why stop with Japan?

The door of the Orient had opened wide before me. I would plunge through as into a bright garden. There was China lying ahead of me, and India and Borneo, and Sumatra and Java and all the others, calling me, inviting me.

Circumstances favored me. They favored my traveling by hurting my heart. I returned to America with my husband, only to find that our life together was not advisable. We agreed to separate, and the divorce followed shortly. That is not an interesting story.

The earlier day that I set sail in my own ex-missionary ship, alone, for the South Seas, an eager, bewildered little girl on a lark, was not more exciting to me than that day some years later when I left the Golden Gate once more, in a steamer, for Hong Kong. There was a sense of finality about it. On my first escapade I had been "through with love and men." This time I was even more "through." Marriage I had tried, and tried rather fully. The Sea of Matrimony, the "young girl's birthright," had no glamor for me. I had also had enough of Western ideas, of Western forms and principles and conventions. I would go back and into that glorious, age-old East, which was rich in thought before Greece, before Rome, before Egypt, and where millions upon millions of yellow men spend a lifetime seeking the philosophy of that lifetime.

There is one incident of that trip which must be told, for it was the first time in my life that I came into contact with crime. But I fear I shall have to distort my story slightly, for the crime was in all the papers, and the criminal is still alive. I do not, at my age, wish to be held as material witness after-the-fact in a case which flared and died over thirty years ago.

It begins with dinner on the first day out.

Sitting at my table were two very unusual-looking persons, man and wife. He was about 65 years old, was possessed of one of the most beautiful faces I had ever seen on any male, beautiful in spite of whitening gray hair. His meticulously trained and combed mustachios which, over the merest *zeste* of a goatee, classed him immediately to anyone who knew the Southwest. He was of that fine rare type who settled in Southern California, grew to money and power, and built for themselves something which resembled a little feudal state.

He was Spanish. His name was something like Don José d'Almeida y Calledos. He wore a costume that accentuated the grand air of dignity which was naturally his ... black velvet jacket and silken stock. His English was accurate, but tinged with a slight accent.

But his wife was even more astounding.

She had green eyes.

When I say "green," I do not mean gray-green nor greenish nor anything but sheer emerald hue. I have never since seen anything like it. And they contrasted with the vivid copper-red hair, a skin as white as wax, and the exquisitely carved features of the unmistakable aristocrat . . . or the supposedly unmistakable aristocrat.

But Donna d'Almeida was no Spanish lady. She was an American from New Orleans, as I soon discovered in conversation, and she was only 35 years of age. Furthermore, there was something about her . . . I could not for the life of me have defined it . . . that was out of tune. I took it to be some trick of her strange eyes . . . but you shall see.

On the fifth day of our long voyage, Don José did not appear for dinner. He was indisposed, his wife told me. And she and I were drawn more than ever into conversation. More than ever I felt that there was something strange about the woman, but I liked her. She was unusual, and far more than handsome.

Next day, Don José appeared – but how changed. Drawn and yellow, he seemed really to be suffering. I asked him, naturally, if he had had the ship's medical service, but he said not, and that his wife was taking care of him as well and better than any ship's doctor could.

Thereafter his appearances were more and more irregular, and each time he seemed to look more like a handsome cadaver than the last. One night, about five days before reaching Hong Kong, the Green-Eyed Woman came to my stateroom as I was preparing for bed. She was tense. She was evidently "in a state."

"Can I trust you?" she asked me bluntly.

I told her that she could, and my curiosity was bubbling over.

"I don't mean in the ordinary way," she parried. "But suppose I should confide something really terrible in you? Could I trust you?"

She had me there. Nothing could have determined me more quickly.

"Well," she said panting, and obviously on the edge of her nerves, "I must tell somebody. I shall go mad."

"Well?"

"My husband is dying. He will be dead before we reach Hong Kong."

That would ordinarily have aroused me, but I knew that he was ill. She had led me to expect more than this.

"I was afraid he was ill. Was that what you wanted to say?"

But her long green eyes glowed through their curved slits, peering into my eyes.

"Not entirely," she said. Then she burst out with: "He's dying of poison. He's meant to die. Now do you understand?"

I did not.

"No? What do you mean?"

"I'm poisoning him. I'm murdering him if you want to call it that. Now you know."

She sat there like gilded ivory, staring into the blank wall of my stateroom. I did not know what to say. Nor what to do. Finally I asked:

"Why?"

"I want his money. I married him for it five years ago, and he will never die unless I make him. Just that. No other reason. Now you can give me away to the Captain if you want."

And with that she got up quickly and walked out, slamming the door as though I had done her a personal injury.

Murder!

If this were not madness, a hallucination . . . if it were true, then, technically, I would be just as much of a murderess as she

~ 136 ~

was. I ought to tell the Captain. I even quite convinced myself that I was going to do so.

But I never did. I cannot explain why. I could not have done it.

In two days the handsome old man was dead.

"Phthisis" was the verdict, if I remember rightly. He was buried at sea.

And that night, after the burial, his red-haired, green-eyed widow came to me ... not to thank me, but to say:

"You murderess! Why did you let me do it? ..." and words to that effect, in such a fury and in such a state of wild resentment of the fact that I should have permitted her to carry on, that I was bewildered. But I saw that she was not herself. I both despised her and felt sorry for her. And I was afraid of her, to be truthful. She was like some reincarnation of an ancient Egyptian cat-woman. I left her raving in my stateroom and went on deck. Two hours later, when I came back, she had gone.

She was met in Hong Kong, at the pier, by a young Englishman.

I learned later that she had purchased one of the finest residences on "the peak" and that they were both squandering Don José's ill-inherited money.

Women have always been a mystery to me, a woman.

CHAPTER XVII

A New Vice: Opium Dens in France,
an illustration from *Le Petit Journal*, 1903.

B ut let us get on to China and things more pleasant.

Hong Kong, when I reached it, was as Sino-British as you please. England had "leased" it from the Chinese Empire about 1830, which really means that the Chinese Emperor had been afraid not to "lease it."

Immigration authorities were British. Police were Sikhs. Porters were Chinese, Cingalese, Korean ... what-have-you. And the whole place, a little colony-city of some 300,000 yellow souls, not to mention the 15,000 or more white souls, was fantastically unbelievable.

The harbor was like a lake. Blue-marine for ten miles, overshadowed by the Peak and the high Kowloon peninsula.

Somebody aptly said once that it is Tommy Atkins' farthest sentry-box, and I heard or read somewhere that a British soldier said on being sent there that you couldn't send him any further from home without sending him nearer.

It is true.

That curious, unbelievable city of Hong Kong, a military stronghold, a coaling station for John Bull, teeming and thronging with little yellow men, tall parchment-faced men, fat Mongolians, brown Malays, Hindoos, Parsees, Portuguese, is like a cauldron of broth which the British are skimming.

But it is beautiful.

The beauty is not like that of Japan. There are none of the charming little gardens with red bridges. You do not have the sensation of stage scenery. But you feel the age. Centuries of age. In the tree, in the sky, in the good sunshine, in the moldering fogs.

I think my first impression was a nasal one.

I *smelled* Hong Kong before I ever left the big white boat. I heard a clamor, I felt a pressure, I sensed age and old power. The East was there, slightly tinged with the West, slightly cleaned up and made presentable for British officers and their wives. But it was the East. I was in it. I was plunging.

In Japan you ride in 'rickishas. In China you ride in chairs. The Sedan-chair is an institution, not for speed as is the rickshaw, but especially designed to flatter the vanity of the occupant. It is easy to imagine oneself a queen in a chair.

My hotel was on the Peak. That eminence is about two miles south of Victoria, the English military city, and lifts its snobbish head about 1800 feet into the blue heavens. There is (or was) a cable tramway, and your first ride is a new sort of intoxication because all the houses seem to be falling over and drunken.

The purser contrived to get my baggage into the hands of not more than three coolies and arranged a price that was not robbery. I also got me into a chair and the chair tottered with me as far as the tram and the tram managed to deposit me on the higher level, and my baggage managed to arrive hours later, God knows how.

I had been advised by some one to live on the Peak; I have no other excuse for this absurdity.

Things always happen to me.

They began almost immediately happening in Hong Kong, but before I go into that it might be well to make a little picture of what I saw there and how I remember it, for of all the cities I have ever visited and under whatever circumstances, that first visit to Hong Kong remains so vivid, so striking, that it seems to me symbolic of all that is China ... and I ought to insist that Hong Kong is no more like the rest of China than Boston is like the rest of America.

Hong Kong is crowded. My expression is too mild: it is teeming. I was conscious of more persons living and breathing and "being" about me each moment than had ever lived and breathed and "been" about me before in my life. They were yellow, brown, black, gray, white, olive and back to yellow again. Curious, but there were few women. Men of all shapes and sizes thronged the narrow streets of the Asiatic city, but women were in a huge minority. Why? I found out later.

It appears that the Chinese population of Hong Kong is largely Cantonese, and that the careful gentlemen from Canton leave their wives at home for two reasons. Number One: they do not trust the morals of the blond foreigner, be he British, an officer-and-gentleman, or merely a gentleman. Perhaps they have learned from Mr. Atkins. Number Two: It is cheaper to leave wives at home. A pretty good explanation, when you think of it.

I said a little above that in China you take chairs, not 'rikishas. It is not quite true. There are the fast little runners (Japanese, too) to be found in Hong Kong, although very few. I remember them distinctly, because it was in a Hong Kong 'rikisha that I got my first shock of contrast here. I had been shopping. Of that more later, for whoever concocted the legal-latin "caveat emptor" must have done some shopping in Hong

Kong . . . no longer on the Peak, by the way. I found a 'rikisha, babbled pidgin, and got under way at a great pace.

The streets grew narrower, dirtier, more picturesque, if one can call it that. And more fragrant. Sewers had not taken root in old China, despite the admirable attempts of the British. Narrower, dirtier, more filled with draping signs in all colors and gold, crowded with little yellow men in black shirts and slippers and sleeves, with big yellow men the same, with tottering women . . . only a few children, animals of various sorts, darker and dingier and more fetid.

And then, just at the minute I believed it was going to end in something more awful and more romantic than I had ever dreamed, the light burst in upon me and the fairer streets, cleaner and policed, the British city, surrounded me.

Curious impression.

Curious contrast.

"Never the twain shall meet," suggested the poet. You almost believe him to be a liar, and yet . . .

Indian soldiers in their brilliant turbans draped themselves about. (They didn't drape, exactly, but they were as decorative as drapings.) Sikh policemen looked very businesslike, efficient and contented. A tramway made its presence known, as though thumbing its nose at the ancient ways. And, in the midst of this extraordinary mixture of races and thought and purposes, there was a stall or tiny two-by-four shed which contained one Buddhist priest with an iron bar over three feet long thrust through his cheeks, blood streaming, bearing his pain with perfect composure, an object lesson to passersby.

I learned that the priest submitted publicly to this self-torture in order to stimulate people into contributing to his temple which needed repairs. "If I can suffer thus, you can deprive yourself of a little . . ." That was the meaning.

I guess we in the West know very little of what true religious fervor is.

A little bit more description.

Society in Victoria was conducted on the military plan. The Governor, two Admirals, a General, a Chief Justice and the Anglican Bishop were the leaders. Tiffin was a great daytime function. Dancing, gambling, drinking and things of even lesser moral worth filled the night.

It is almost miraculous how we Anglo-Saxons can keep our Right Hands from consciousness of the deeds of our Left Hands. I wonder how it is that the Captains Sir Reginald Humpty-Blye-Blye, so austere and so military, can keep face with themselves. I don't mean this to be a strict reference to the British. Hong Kong *is* British, but the same self-hiding goes on in Shanghai, Peking and other places, with Americans setting the pace.

For instance . . .

This story is by way of a confession; you can take it or leave it and you can judge it as you please.

I was about to leave Hong Kong when a certain young officer who had demonstrated a rather more than lukewarm interest in me, decided that my education was lacking and that he should show me the "underworld" of Hong Kong.

Little I knew.

We had danced and he had done some drinking.

(I ought to have mentioned that on my last trip home I had promised my mother that I would never drink alcohol in any form again. I never did. Otherwise I should not be alive to write this book.) We danced, he drank, we wandered.

We took a chair to a section of the city I had never even heard of, much less seen.

There was, in a street so narrow you could touch each side, and so dirty you could only use a bottle of smelling salts in defense, a weird sort of house built in five tiers and capped, each tier, like a pagoda. It being later than midnight, there was no one on the street, but somehow you felt conscious of people being near you.

There was a door. Its appearance was not that of an unusual door, but it had nevertheless a certain presence. Captain X. rapped sharply after talking in Chinese with his private chair bearers. The door suddenly vanished. It flew upwards into space without a sound.

A single lantern burned dimly in a plain, uninteresting room. We went in, and the door came back from space and closed upon us, still without a sound. At the end of the room a curtain of heavy, rather dirty yellow silk moved aside, and a fat Cingalese bowed over his folded hands, indicating a stairway.

My captain apparently knew his way, and escorted me downstairs. Below I could hear vague sounds suggesting music. I could also hear more knocking on the upstairs door. More visitors.

The room below was less plain, covered by several straw mats, but unfurnished. Another curtain, another Cingalese, and another stair. We descended, and then the music was plainer and a vague *flair* of aromatic smoke greeted us. A long, brightly lighted passage, draped in silk (clean, this time) and another silken door, and then we found ourselves in an enormous room with an enormous mixture of people in it in various positions.

I suppose to you of the younger generation who know your

night-clubs and your Chinatown-for-fifty-cents tours this may seem all very tame.

But those things were unknown, especially to young women in their twenties, in those days, and I am willing to admit right here that I was not only impressed but also a little alarmed. It was plainly "not nice." There was nothing in the room upon which you could put your finger and say "this will not do," but there was a certain air which the French might call *"louche."*

A modern roulette table centered the room. There were women. There were men. There were rich costumes, oriental and European. There seemed to be a certain tension, though that may have been imaginary.

Nobody noticed us except four oily Chinamen in gorgeous colors who seemed to be the principals of the establishment, and who acted like over-eager tradesmen expecting us to buy something.

Captain X. knew many. He saluted and was greeted in return. I was introduced to several groups, but we did not stay in the roulette room.

Passing through and under more of the inevitable curtains, we found ourselves in another large room whose atmosphere was quite different. Music came from somewhere ... Chinese music, full of weird harmonies and weirder discords. But it was very soft. In the diminished light I became conscious that the room was more than really a room but had alcoves made of draperies all about it and that these alcoves had people in them.

Seated on mats here and there were solitary figures, Chinese, smoking pensively, not talking, not seeing.

"This is called vice," said my Officer-and-Gentleman.

Opium.

But my guide had other things in mind. We did not inspect more closely the people whose souls were floating far away in some opiate dreamland, but went down another stairway, this time rather splendid and decorated in gold lacquer and with grotesque and beautiful carvings.

Another mixture of races greeted us.

Tables distinctly un-Chinese were conveniently arranged round the most curious room I have ever seen. The floor was carpeted thickly and richly, black and gold was the note in colored lacquer over the heavy carved beams that braced the ceiling, arched slightly, and suggestive of the interior of a pagoda. (I had, at that time, never seen the interior of a pagoda.)

At the tables sat the army, and with them, drinking tea and other liquids, were silken little girls, chiefly Chinese, but with many a blond head among them, in low and intimate conversation.

We were seated. We were served. We scarcely talked.

I was nervous and rather embarrassed. I was soon to be more so.

In one corner of the room was a table which seemed rather more noticeable than the others because the talk was louder and there had been more liquids served.

As we took our places, a young man in evening clothes saw my captain and got up, rather shakily, to greet him. There was a brief introduction, and my guide excused himself for a moment and went over to the other table, leaving me alone.

I had not been alone for more than a few minutes when the palace was frozen by a scream, the long, agonizing, heart-rending scream of a woman.

The Anglo-Saxon faction was electrified. Men stood to their

feet. The Chinese fat-gentleman who smoked lazily on a plat-form at one end of the room merely puffed his pipe.

Then the curtains which concealed the stairs we had just come down were thrust aside, and something walked slowly through.

It was a woman.

She was so blond that at first sight she seemed an albino, or to be wearing a powdered wig. She walked stiffly, frozenly, her eyes fixed straight ahead. And in her beautiful face, in her wide staring eyes, there was a horror such as I have never imagined could be expressed in the human features.

Then without warning and before anyone could shake off the tension that held us all, she screamed again.

She threw back her head, threw her arms out and up, and screamed, and then fell in a heap on the floor, moaning and making plaintive little sounds expressive of mental agony.

The fat Chinaman blew smoke in her direction.

Seven Anglo-Saxons rushed to her. At their touch she screamed the louder.

"Go away, you dirty ——s."

The little girls stopped their drinking and their chatter to look at her, each one with her own rather superior manner.

I couldn't stand it. I got up and went over to her and laid my hand on her shoulder and spoke to her.

"Can I help?" I asked, or something like that.

Perhaps it was my voice . . . something had an effect on her like cold water. She stopped writhing and looked up at me, breathing hard. There was surprise in her face, and wonder.

"Get away from here, for God's sake," she whispered.

"I'm sorry. I meant to help. You are in trouble . . ."

She sat up there on the floor, puzzled. She stared at me . . .

There was a group around us by this time, but she did not see the rest.

"Jesus, what are you doing here? You're only a kid ... only a kid."

My captain came back to his post. He pressed my shoulder.

"We'd better go," he said.

"Yes, go. Take her out of here, you damned fool," said the girl. "What did you bring her here for?"

I might have answered that I was able to take care of myself ... not that it was true. I might also have told my captain coldly that I was going to take this girl out of the place, for I had some such vague idea. But another person stepped through the silk doorway and everything changed.

It was a man. A Chinese man.

He was over six foot and a half, and dressed European fashion. He looked unsmilingly at the people, at me, and then at the girl.

"Hysterics?" he asked, coldly.

She jumped at his voice, stared at him, but said nothing.

"Stop being maudlin, Bonny," he said to her, in perfect English. "You're interrupting business again. Ah Feng won't like it."

And then, to the rest:

"She tried the 'cure,' and you can see what shape her nerves are in. She's not dangerous. Merely pities herself."

The girl was trembling and staring at the tall Chinaman in real terror. She clung to me, and I put my arm around her.

Then I became conscious of the man in another way.

His eyes seemed two inches long ... I have never seen anything like it. His nose was not of the type usual in China, but straight and well formed. His chin was firm and square and his forehead broad and high. He had a commanding presence which everybody in the room could feel.

He stood there, looking at me, now. It made me feel almost as I had felt years before under the hypnotic spell of Washington Irving Bishop in Honolulu. The man had power. He was mysterious as though wearing a mask, and he had power.

"I wouldn't waste my time with her if I were you," he said to me, and then turned to my guide. "I have a chair outside if you think you had better take the young lady home, Captain X. May I . . . ?"

By now I had regained my speech.

"Thank you," I said, "but we have a chair. And I'm taking this poor girl with me."

She gripped me tightly.

He stared coldly at me, and then said just as coldly:

"Ah? But she is under contract to this place. She is worth one thousand Mex."

We Californians die hard.

"I'll pay it. To whom?"

He looked at me evenly, while Captain X. mumbled protests and something about the proprieties. Then he answered me.

"Ah Feng is here and will naturally permit you to throw your money away, but I think it is a trifle foolish."

His poise and nonchalance were maddening.

Then he spoke rapidly in Chinese, and the Chinese fat-gentleman came clambering down from his perch on the platform, bowing and smirking and trying to say something in English, which, to my ears, was as good as Chinese.

I produced a checkbook on the Shanghai correspondents of my bank, and made out a check to cash, for 1000 dollars Mex.

It made a sensation, I can tell you, but I felt like the heroine of a melodrama.

As I held it out, the girl on the floor snatched it and crumpled it up, crying:

"No, no, no, you damned fool, you can't do that . . ."

But the fat Chinaman was on her in a moment and with a twist of his hand had her helpless, the check falling on the floor in a ball. He grabbed it, smoothed it out, scrutinized it, and put it in his pocket, smiling and bowing and scraping. Then he went back to his platform and pipe.

"Now, Bonny, you are free," said the tall Chinaman. "Thank the lady."

She looked up at me, crying huge tears and shaking her head. I lifted her to her feet, took the arm of my rather bewildered and not-a-little-shocked captain, and pushed the blond girl through the silk door. I had had enough.

As we went through, I heard the tall Chinaman's voice say:

"Rather indiscreet of you, Captain X.," and I could feel my cavalier's muscles tighten in anger. But he said nothing.

Outside, he said:

"My God, I never should have taken you there. Damned drunken idea of mine. Please forgive me."

I tried to tell him I did not mind and that I was glad I could help the girl, but he had no enthusiasm about her either. I could see that.

As for the girl, she said almost nothing. She asked where I was taking her, and I told her to my hotel. We were carried along in silence, and very slowly, she making extra weight in the chair. Finally Captain X. spoke:

"You remember the Chinaman? The one in evening dress?"

Before I could answer, the girl spoke up.

"If you do, forget him. I'll kill him one day."

Now all this was very confusing and bewildering to me, and I wanted to know just what it was that had happened and who the Chinaman was. The girl and the captain seemed to have a mutual tacit understanding not to tell me, and they put me off with ridiculous remarks, chiefly warning me against the big Celestial.

Of course, nothing could have excited my curiosity more. But for the moment I did not press the thing.

At my hotel the captain left us, rather reluctantly, and I took the girl to my rooms, making some sort of explanation to the hotel clerk.

"Now, tell me about it," I asked her. After much begging the question she did.

Her name was Bonny Walke. She had come to China four years before, married to a missionary. That was ironical. One day while trying to get into Manchuria with her husband and a party, they were attacked by bandits and she was held for ransom with a young missionary and hidden outside of Changsha in Hunan somewhere. They almost died of cold and starvation, but the two of them eventually escaped. Well, according to her a natural intimacy grew up between the young missionary and herself. She made a hero of him. But she insisted that there was nothing out of the way. Her story goes that her missionary husband, who managed not to be caught by the bandits, did not see the platonic relationship in quite the same light, and that he was jealous of their continued friendship when they got back to Shanghai. Anyhow, he left her, and she was in disgrace socially. She tried various jobs, and finally came to Hong Kong as the companion of a young American girl who was very rich.

The girl met the big Chinaman I had seen, fell in love with him and married him. She died six months afterwards, and he got all her money. He, it appears, was a Manchurian noble and a lawyer of some note, but enjoyed rather a bad reputation in the British settlement. Bonny Walke insisted that he had poisoned his American wife, that he had also poisoned a former rich Chinese wife, and that he was the owner of all the vice-dens in all the foreign settlements of China. In fact she said so much about him that I began to believe it was impossible for any man, Chinese or not, to be as bad as she said he was. And so very good-looking, too.

But that was Bonny Walke's story and she stuck to it.

You will be amused to know that I later learned quite differently. She was never a missionary's wife, had come over with an entertainment troupe on a Pacific liner and had taken a job as "hostess" at one of the Shanghai gambling establishments, had gone in for opium and had turned out the wreck of a beautiful girl that I saw.

But give her credit for imagination.

I saw the Chinaman again. This you expected from the foregoing, but I doubt if you expected the real circumstances.

Let me say right here and now that I never was a woman to "follow up" a man. In fact, as nearly as I can remember I have never even telephoned a man in my life. It is not any false idea of superiority nor yet any purposeful trick to make them come to me. Yet the fact remains. Analyzing it, I suppose I am too lazy. Or it is because I have always clung to the old-fashioned idea that Man is the pursuer and Woman the pursued. I like gallantry. I have always liked it. And it leaves very little place for gallantry if the woman takes the role of the pursuer, whatever the form or the excuse may be.

But to my story.

I had gone to Macao, the Brilliant, and it was a Sunday. This is a place about three hours from Hong Kong by steamer where the whole world comes to gamble. By that I mean, of course, the whole Western world gathered in the East.

In the company of an English lieutenant and some friends I inspected the famous place and ventured even to play a little myself, although I have never been lucky at games of chance. Suddenly I heard myself paged. I thought it was a mistake, but no. It was quite real.

Responding, I learned that a gentleman had come all the way from Hong Kong in a private yacht to see me on some special matter, but the "boy" (he was fifty if a day) could tell me no more. Curiosity overcoming discretion, I followed my "boy," and suddenly found myself face to face with the tall Celestial.

Immaculate and intensely European in attire, he stood in the bar, bowing with extreme Oriental courtesy.

"I fear I have taken advantage of you," were his first words.

Rather dazed, I assured him that he had not. Little I knew.

"I called at your hotel," he went on, "and learned that you had come here. I followed you. Was I rude? You Americans, one never knows."

It left me little to say. Again I assured him to the contrary.

"My only excuse is perhaps difficult to explain," he went on. "You are a . . . a type. You are curiously interested in people. One could not help but observe. I could find no one who was willing to present me formally. You see, I enjoy rather a bad reputation. So I took the liberty . . ."

It was about like that. The words I do not remember exactly. Mr. Huan Kai Chan was a contrast to most of the men

I had met in my life. He did not have the air I had so frequently observed of looking for a comfortably well-to-do wife. He seemed to need nothing. He was self-sufficing. His words seemed to be proven by his attitude . . . interested in me as a "type."

Well, in revenge, I was interested in him as a "type."

Can you imagine anything so beautiful? Tall beyond most tall men, copper-colored, full lips, deep eyes of that extraordinary length, full, rounded chin, erect, king-like, the image of what you have always conceived to be meant by a Chinese Prince. Not noticeably Oriental, exquisitely dressed, poised . . .

But why go on? He was fascinating.

I scarcely remember how he did it, but conversation grew and I suddenly found myself walking aboard his yacht, quite at ease, quite his guest, quite unafraid of his bad reputation which he admitted so readily, so gracefully, so apologetically.

And I had forgotten about the nice, sturdy English lieutenant.

There is no good in trying to explain what happened.

I fell under the spell of Huan Kai Chan, under the spell of his Manchurian mystery, his power, his princeliness. That was all.

And I did not return from his yacht for three weeks.

It was like stepping into a new world. Modern, the yacht, and yet there was something about the teakwood finishing, the rich silks, the constantly burning incense, that dated ten thousand years before the Scottish builders of that steam powerplant and hull were born.

And there was something about the crew.

Discipline was the word. It was not like the military discipline of American or European conception. It was fear and respect. There was no form you could see. There was no ritual.

But there was a feeling that every gesture, every clap of the hands would be obeyed . . . to the letter.

And so they were.

There was something about Huan Kai, as I always called him, that reminded one of the Count of Monte Cristo. Magnificence. Abundance. The grand manner.

And yet, never a smile, never the slightest betrayal of emotion. He was a man absolutely apart from others. What torrents of thought went on behind that beautiful Oriental mask, no one ever knew. Least of all I.

He had a habit of sitting all morning, nearly rigid, on a mat, robed in glorious silks of brilliant color, looking either straight ahead of him or straight at me. Not a word was spoken. Not a line of his face moved.

He did not smile, but he could tell stories, and he could tell me about his amazing country. I think I never have known anybody who could be so fascinating in description of a country as Huan Kai was. He loved China, admired even its poor struggle to maintain its place in a world which had surpassed it in mechanical devices as a substitute for civilization. But most of all he loved her traditions and her age-old thought and philosophy which we cheaply call religions.

Whatever Huan Kai may have been to the outside world, that, for reasons which were probably well founded, gave him the title of "Mr. Gold," he was a man of unfathomable culture and erudition. I even grew to be afraid of him, like everybody else, but I never ceased to admire his mind and his learning.

"Remarkable man, but a swine," was the comment of a certain British officer. It was entirely true.

But I am getting ahead of my story.

I want to paint for you some of the insight Huan Kai gave me to Chinese life. I never could have learned it otherwise, for I am not one of those who learn languages easily and Chinese remained always a closed book to me.

Perhaps the thing which Americans and Europeans have the greatest difficulty in understanding about Orientals is their attitude towards women. At least it is true of the missionaries we send there. I may be wrong, but I think that more effort has been devoted by divers branches of the Christian Church to uproot concubinage in China than any of the so-called evils which are supposed to prevail there.

Far be it from me to approve or disapprove the system. But let me explain it to you as Huan Kai explained it to me.

In the Chinese household, the mother-in-law is supreme. The wife awaits only the day she may become one and so come, in her turn, into power. I mean, naturally, the mother of the husband. A man has seven reasons for divorcing his wife, the first and most important being disobedience to his mother. A Chinese woman has no legal grounds for divorce, since she cannot obtain one without her husband's permission.

The result of this arrangement is curious. It works two ways. First, it tends to cultivate a philosophical acceptance of life on the part of married women. Homes, in general, are happier than in our Western world. Secondly, every family desires male children rather than female children. Not only that they may be heirs, but so that the wife may hold her position of authority.

In cases where the children are continually girls, there is great unhappiness. The wife, in self-defense, "eats vinegar," as the saying is, which means that she either procures a mistress for her husband or welcomes (ostensibly) a mistress of his own choosing.

If the mistress has children, male or female, it is the legitimate wife who is their "mother," and the mistress is called "nurse." This is very important to the home and to family life, for barrenness is another reason for divorce in China, and the mistress may often serve to keep the family united.

There at least is a sort of insight into the soul of China that Huan Kai gave me. I am grateful for it, whatever it be worth.

Another thing was his deep comprehension of the religious meaning of his country. Himself, he was a Buddhist, but his understanding of the other three . . . if they may thus be called . . . doctrines or systems . . . was complete.

He knew Christianity, not as a religion, but as a philosophical system. He had read the Bible, had traveled in Europe and in America and had even studied in some of the world's most famous universities. And his favorite theme was that no religion was ever created by the West, and that all the doctrines of the world came from Oriental sources. Christianity is but a revised form of Judaism, he pointed out, and its forms and rites are adaptations of Oriental cults.

Yes, I admired Huan Kai. All these things and more he talked of to me, in that slow, almost inattentive manner of his. He seemed to take a pride in teaching me and explaining to me the meaning of his country and his countrymen. And I was grateful, in a girlish way, although I was not and never have been the scholarly sort of woman.

But there was a miracle at work in me . . . the miracle that I had never understood on that early day when I had a vision of the Hindoo woman on my childhood bed. The East and its subtle spirit were filling me and working in me and reaching out to me and calling me. I was in tune with those things which

Westerners can seldom comprehend altogether and generally not at all. I am sure that Huan Kai knew it and that it was part of his entire scheme about me.

But now the scene changes. Hong Kong and its British Victoria, its Cantonese wifeless population, its Peak and its Turkish bath rainstorms ... and the well-meaning, nice, but somehow "heavy" English captain whose attentions were beginning to be boring ... all of this changed and slipped behind, and I dropped splash into the heart of China, into the soul of China, and my own soul was filled with it.

We went to Shanghai.

The mere fact of going to another Chinese city may not seem like much of importance if you have never been to Shanghai, but let me insist upon it. Shanghai is like no other city in the world. I will not use the old word "astounding," but it is hard to avoid it, for that ancient city (named Shanghai "on the sea," by a forgotten emperor) is, or was in that day, a place to astound anyone.

Huan Kai and I embarked in his yacht and sailed into the port of the Wangpoo River, winding our way amongst the junks and sampans and through the smells and noises into Shanghai. As in Yokohama, the waterfront is called the Bund, and a magnificent thoroughfare it is. The foreign settlement was not very impressive to me, for I was in search of Chinese reality. But when I was installed in the Oriental Hotel, the only good institution of its kind not distinctly "foreign," I perceived that even here I was in the midst of the Orient.

My room is worth a description.

The only partitions were thin green wooden panels which reached just to the top of the door. At night a brilliant light from the outer hallway shone in and made sleeping impossible . . . until you got used to it. Not only that, but on the roof was a Chinese orchestra, composed of cats, whistles, cicadas, tin pans, crickets, sandpaper and combs with tissuepaper over them . . . or so I conceived it. They played and wailed and screeched until midnight or later, and, as if they were an accompaniment, passers-by on the famous Nanking Road talked politics or some other subject which required a vigor that was truly Celestial.

In the hallways also there was talk . . . real, argumentative talk with that peculiar rise and fall and inflection of voices which the Chinese language demands . . . and *fortissimo!*

Sleep finally did visit me out of sheer exhaustion, but in the early morning the songs of the coolies, pushing wheelbarrows and busy at other such jobs, brought me out of it in no good mood. The sons of Han are a noisy race.

But my hotel life was not a long one. Huan Kai owned a house in the reaches of the native city where we went as soon as it was properly opened to receive us. And there began my ostracism from the foreign colony.

For it was an indiscretion even to mention the native city, much less to go there. It is a peculiar sort of snobbery that only Anglo-Saxons abroad could conceive.

So my indiscretions began.

I remember very well my first entry into the mysteries of Shanghai. We had formed a longish train of 'rikishas, and our own rubber-tired carriage in the lead and five others following with baggage and necessaries, in charge of Huan Kai's body servant. The more or less modern buildings of the foreign city became older and more Chinese as the edges neared. Then we passed through a wall and everything changed.

We entered the "Street of Ivory Carvers."

On both sides of this gap among age-old buildings were the stalls and booths where the members of one of the most glorious trade-guilds in China were creating their white marvels. An elephant's tusk became a work of delicate lace, a knife handle, a complicated box that only you could open, a set of Mah-Jong . . . you know the sort of things. But how different from seeing them in the rue de la Paix.

There were walls, and walls within walls. Beggars as filthy as you can imagine crowded your 'rikishas, screamed and bleated, withered and maimed and leprous and pitted with disease. Horrible. There were all kinds of shops and booths, leaning and huddling together, hanging with a million signs glittering with Chinese characters. We passed a courtyard where they made Sedan-chairs and through a street so narrow that two of these could never pass each other. And all around us, slipping along in dragging shoes, gleaming as to their polished hair or pointed hats, were men and women and naked boys and little girls, that spelled for me all the romance I had ever imagined.

But that was nothing. It was only the emotion of an impressionable young girl spinning tapestries out of her imagination.

In the heart of a courtyard, the core of tangled, jumbled little streets, was the house of Huan Kai. It was immense. It was of brick, with its glazed tile roof, the corners curled and pointing upwards like any Chinese house, to be sure that the evil spirits of the air, who can only follow a straight line, would not alight in the courtyard.

CHAPTER XVIII

Shanghai street scene, 1910.

A door opened for us, magically and mysteriously.
We went in.
I was in prison.

Huan Kai's house was a palace. I doubt if the wealthiest and most powerful mandarin in Shanghai had anything to equal it. But in spite of the magnificent lacquer paneling, in spite of the jade and the incense and the ivory, it was a prison. I felt it upon entering, and it was as if I had been somehow betrayed.

Can you imagine a young American suddenly finding herself the mistress of a household containing over one hundred servants, as many rooms, furnished with a luxury that baffles words, and all of it centering round a strange, huge, silent man, who never smiled, never laughed, and whose sternness was apparent from the way his battery of servants jumped at the slightest lift of his eyes?

Life began on the second night. A dinner party. And what a dinner party! The preparation was for fifteen people, and it was then that I learned just how far Oriental magnificence can go.

Huan Kai was like a feudal lord. He was a legend in Shanghai. At these dinner parties he even dictated the costumes that should be worn by his guests ... he prepared gorgeous silk robes for them to wear, and every one had his own color, his own design, in rich, glorious material, ready for him when he arrived.

On this night, everybody was to dress in brilliant green, and Huan Kai had favors of jade, curiously and beautifully carved flasks of solid jade. It was stunning. It was entirely beyond me.

And on this night I had a warning of the future.

One of the guests was a charming young Russian nobleman who was in Shanghai on some diplomatic mission. He spoke Chinese fluently, but no English. I suppose that since I was the only woman present, it was perfectly natural that all the guests should be attentive to me, and the Russian discovered that I could speak a little French, so he started one of these polite conversations. It was a relief, for however brilliant the talk may have been in Chinese, I understood not one little word of it.

After dinner, I went away from the group just for a moment. I had had barely time to mount the stairs and enter my own room before the other door opened sharply, and there stood Huan Kai. He had evidently left the diners a second after I did, and had come up by the stairs in the left wing.

"Li-ti," he said in his soft, even vibrating voice ... (he had given me that sweet little Chinese name ... "Li-ti"), "there is one thing that is to be remembered. I am the master of all that is beautiful in this house, and I, Huan Kai Chan, may keep those things, or give them away, or break them, if it pleases me. Do not forget that, Li-ti."

Then he calmly walked out.

I was astounded. What did he mean? Little by little I began to have a glimmer of understanding. Huan Kai was, in some ridiculous way, jealous of the Russian who had been making polite conversation in French with me. I will admit that at first it rather dazed me, and then that it really amused me.

If I had had any common sense, I would have seen the writing on the wall. But I was too vain, too young and self-confident to realize exactly what might come out of such unreasonable jealousy. I learned.

In fact, I went downstairs and flirted a little with the Russian as a sort of lark . . . just to see if I could make the somber Manchu change the expression on his masklike face.

I couldn't. He didn't. But towards the end of the evening he came over to me as I was chatting in my bad French, and said:

"Li-ti, I have imagined a most interesting plan for you tomorrow. The notorious bandit Ling Wing-pu is to be questioned at the prison. I will take you to the ceremony. It is a curiosity."

And again he walked straight away, leaving the young Russian looking at him in complete amazement.

"Mon Dieu!" he exclaimed. "But he can't mean . . ."

He did not finish, and although I pressed him he would say nothing more.

I was getting more and more bewildered. I had no idea of why Huan Kai should want me to hear a trial in Chinese, or whatever it was, and yet I felt somehow that it had something to do with this silly and meaningless flirtation I was carrying on. And later I saw my Russian talking earnestly to Huan Kai, pleading, making gestures, while that big Manchu body stood towering over him, arms folded, expressionless, saying not one word.

No, it was all too mysterious.

The next day the mystery grew still further, and a little horror was added to make it more complete.

I had almost forgotten about Huan Kai's promise to take

me to the prison, but one of the hundred servants came to my quarters and with much ceremony and much difficulty made me understand that the "All Powerful One" was awaiting me. The old woman Meh-ki, my personal servant, then appeared, and with her ten younger servants, all carrying silks and Chinese robes of every kind. I learned that I was expected to costume myself as becomes a woman of high station in China. I did not mind, naturally, and if ever I achieved beauty in my life ... and occasionally men, in a romantic mood, have mentioned something about it ... I did it at that moment. There is nothing Chinese or Oriental in my features, but when I looked into the broad mirror that three of the girls held for me, I failed to recognize myself. It may have been unreal and theatrical, but it was certainly beautiful.

I was a proud little girl when I presented myself before Huan Kai and saw his long, full eyes sparkle.

Like feudal lord and lady, we were ushered into our gold-encrusted, lacquered Sedan-chair, and were immediately surrounded by servants in gorgeous livery. We moved out of the courtyard into the twisted, narrow streets of Shanghai like a little army. I was very much impressed.

But there was something about Huan Kai that had changed. His silence was nothing new nor his austerity. But some sort of change had come over him, and it worried me.

If I were a skillful writer, I might hope to create a shudder and make it tremble through these pages as I recall that day. My memory of it is still tinged with terror ... not a fear of anything defined, but a formless fear for the human race, a realization of the savage in man which persists in spite of his speech, his race, his so-called culture, his customs or his law.

The knot of bearers in their splendid livery were conducting us to the prison. I remember the grimness of it, the rusty brick of its walls, the soldiers in the same style of costume which they had worn for the past five centuries, with their huge swords, and their armor, and metal hats. The prison was a symbol of suppression, of oppression and death.

I remember a courtyard with men crowding around a scaffold. I remember that Huan Kai was greeted on all sides. I was a curiosity, and an uncomfortable one, at that. I recall that I was frightened without knowing why. Perhaps it was that silence, that ominous grimness of Huan Kai.

I will not dwell upon the scene. I cannot.

Briefly: a tall yellow man, so bound with chains that he seemed wrapped into a human cylinder, was carried to the scaffold; was secured to a post, or prop; looked calmly at the gathering below without the least expression on his face. Then a voice from somewhere on the other side of the scaffold began speaking slowly and rhythmically in Chinese. The prisoner, a bandit, or warlord named Ling Wing-pu, turned his head, but otherwise gave no sign of interest. His head was about all he was able to turn.

A little fat Chinaman, with a costume that seemed much too big for him and a sword that certainly was, mounted the platform. Wing Ling-pu never even looked at him. A word of command was given. The Little Chinaman lifted the sword easily . . . and flicked it across the back of the bound man. Red blood followed its path. The unconcerned expression remained on the bandit's face, as though it were somebody else's body that had been cut.

It would drive me mad to record the incidents one by one.

But every time a sing-song voice cried out, and then there was a pause, and then a sharp command, and then the fat torturer made another cut. The bandit became a bloody mess and I was fainting. But I was fascinated: I cannot explain the effect of the scene upon me. Eventually, after countless slices with the huge sword . . . still productive of no expression at all on the face of the tall bound man . . . a vein or artery in the neck was severed and a red fountain played into the air.

That is all I remember. I had to be carried out and taken home.

The most curious thing of all was the expression of satisfaction on the unsmiling face of Huan Kai when I came to.

"We have an amusing way in China, have we not?" he asked me. "It is not given to every American woman to witness the Death of a Thousand Cuts."

I had a vague notion that there was a warning in his remark. You will see later whether I was right.

My life in Shanghai was an odd one, to say the least.

Huan Kai could be very kind, very amusing in his sober way, and very generous in his attitude towards me. Then suddenly he could be cold, despotic and cruel.

For instance, I offended him terribly by a silly and harmless prank to which nobody in the world would have paid any attention except that it was rather undignified.

During one of the great feast periods I managed to escape the eye of the servants and to slip out by myself without Meh-ki, the old woman duenna who was always with me when her master was not. I went down to the river in a hired chair and watched the glorious flower-boats and their pageantry. I thought it would be fun to go on board one of them, but I realized that I could not do so as a foreigner nor as a grande dame of China which I appeared to be when dressed in the native costume. So I returned to the foreign settlement, bought a boy's costume in one of the bazaars, and returned to see the flowers at close range. It was amusing, and perhaps it was not only my imagination that made me feel the coy, solicitous eyes of the girls upon me more than once.

However, when I returned to Huan Kai's palace and slipped in I was caught. He came to my rooms just as I was trying to make a quick change, and I had to tell the truth.

Well, I have never seen such cold fury.

I was afraid he would kill me. He was almost insane. And yet, true to his habits, he scarcely spoke. But I could see from the burning of his eyes and the pressure of his lips that he was on the point of doing me violence.

And on that evening he spent hours trying to make me marry him. From fear, and not from love, I am afraid he was very nearly successful.

But my greatest experience in Shanghai and in all China comes right here. It is not an easy thing to relate. At the risk of shocking Mrs. Grundy I am going to do it, because as far as I know it is unique, although there may possibly be others who have experienced the same thing.

This all sounds mysterious, but it will be explained.

I mentioned that I was ostracized by local European society, less because of my friendship with Huan Kai than because I actually lived in the Chinese city and wore Chinese clothes. I was not entirely shut out, however, and I did have tea with a few friends now and then when I could slip out and take a public chair or 'rikisha over to one of the clubs in the foreign settlement.

It happened on one of those occasions. I had assured myself that Huan Kai was away on business and bribed my duenna, and obeyed that peculiar but rather natural call that one's own race makes.

There is, or was, a famous tea-house in Shanghai which is perhaps better known than any other in the world because it is the model of the Willow Pattern China that every one knows so well. I met two Englishwomen there whom I knew slightly. Now Englishwomen often give the impression that they are very proper and very reserved. But my experience with these two, and a great many after them, has led me to believe that the calm exterior of the British woman conceals something really more adventurous than one ever suspects.

The story begins when I got into conversation with Miss B. and Lady D. Miss B. was telling the story of the Willow Tea-room plate, and it was very sweet and just what I would have expected from the trim, boyish-looking young woman. It is even worth while to repeat it here before going into my adventures, because it contrasts with them so much.

In that very house where the tearoom was, there lived a man with a beautiful daughter whom he wanted to marry to a rich mandarin. But the girl, whose name was Koong Shee, loved Chang, a retainer of her father's. She refused to marry the mandarin, and had to see her lover banished and herself a prisoner on the little lake in the tiny house where the weeping willow can still be seen.

Chang hid in a house the other side of the lake, and sent half a cocoa-nut shell with a little sail in it to carry her a message of his constant love and to invite her to elope with him. She sent the message back that she would, and they did.

Father was angry but the mandarin was more so, and he came and burned the boy's little house where the two had hidden, and their two souls, like doves, floated over the pond for many a day.

Very pretty and very Chinese, but very much unlike what I have got to say now.

Our conversation covered many things, and it came out somehow that I was interested in adventures. Suddenly Lady D. looked steadily through her lorgnette at her friend and said:

"You know, we have just time to take her to the most wonderful of all adventures. Do you think she would care to come?"

Miss B. thought I would, and I protested that I would try anything once. The upshot was that we all hired a chair and away we went to an address that I did not hear. I speak of the fact that we hired a chair, because it was evident that the two English ladies did not want their own bearers to know where they were going.

However, I was not nervous.

After threading through the amazing streets of the old city, we came to a courtyard which was hidden away as if to keep the world from knowing about it, but where there was a very decent-looking house, clean, and seemingly newer than the century-old buildings about it.

My guides got out and went to the door and after pressing on a panel, engaged themselves in conversation with an old woman.

We went in.

I was amazed to see the luxury inside, for the outside of this house, though clean and decent, would never lead one to suspect the richness that it concealed.

The walls were paneled. The paneling was composed of strips of carved ivory, worked into lace-like ornamentation, and bound, every panel, in polished teakwood, likewise carved to frame the beauties of the ivory.

This room was an anteroom, and we sat on two long comfortable benches indicated by the old woman. She in turn left through heavy curtains at the room's further end and left us alone.

I had courage enough to ask my friends what kind of experience was in store for us. I learned little.

"Even if we could tell you," said Lady D., "it would be useless. But you may believe that it is an experience which you will never forget and which, in your turn, you will never be able to describe."

She was right.

She was so right that I hesitate to go further with this feeble attempt at making you understand it. But it has left such an impression on me, and it is so utterly unheard of, in so far as I know, that, after all these years, I am going to try.

The aged attendant returned after a few anxious minutes, and she made my companions understand that all was ready. Lady D. looked at her watch, and insisted that there would not be time for us all to "have the experience" (she constantly used that expression) but that she would withdraw this time so that her friend and I could do so. There was nothing very tense about the place. There was apparently nobody in the house but ourselves, for it was not large and their presence would have been felt or heard. To say that I was bewildered and excitedly curious is putting the case mildly. I was fairly twitching with nervousness.

The two of us were led into another room, also richly furnished, and then up a staircase to one of the most charmingly feminine boudoirs imaginable. Then three young girls in black satin costumes and tight little caps on their heads came in, bringing loose robes. They made us understand that we were to undress and put on the wraps. We did so, I still more nervously, and even Miss B. growing silent and tense.

Then the old woman appeared and beckoned to us.

I insisted that Miss B. go first, and I remember almost better than any other moment in my life the next twenty minutes or so while I sat alone in that strange place, wondering.

I heard almost nothing through the thick curtains that concealed the door through which she had passed, but there was a vague whining sound, like music. It reminded me of a violin, playing far away. Sometimes, when the sound was more distinct, I would feel a slight perspiration and a shiver. It is hard to explain.

After a while, there was dead silence.

Finally I heard the shuffling of slippers, and the curtain was drawn back. It was Miss B. returning.

She was staring straight ahead of her. She did not see me. Her eyes were dilated, her face was flushed. She seemed in a trance. It was as though she had taken a powerful drug. What was it? I almost decided to run away, but the old woman was motioning to me, and I felt obliged to follow her through the door into darkness.

I say darkness. That is not exact. There was the soft glow of a lamp ... a single flame, burning like a soul. It made shadows on the carved ivory panels of the walls. The shadows flickered over a large Chinese bed in the room's center. There was a grass mat on the floor, and absolutely nothing else in the place. The one window back of the bed was covered by an impenetrable curtain. There was not a sound.

The old woman's hands were held out for my robe. Frightened to refuse, I gave it to her, but I was terrified to give it. It seemed as though my last defense . . . against a mysterious, imagined something . . . were being taken away.

She softly pushed me to the bed and motioned me to lie down. I did, as if I were hypnotized. Naked I lay out straight on my back, across the bed. I could see nothing but the flickering shadows of the lamp, and the old woman departing.

Then suddenly there was some one in the room. I had not seen him come in. It was an old man, a very old man, with a thin, wax-like face.

Almost without a sound, he shuffled in silken slippers over towards me, stopped about two yards from the bed, and peered at me in silence. His hands were folded under his large sleeves. His eyes glowed and picked up the light of the lamp from in back of me.

Then, still looking fixedly at me, he unfolded his arms and brought out from somewhere a small stringed instrument with an abnormally long neck. He sat down cross-legged on the floor, turned his back on me, and began to play.

That first note . . . it was as though it were drawn from my heartstrings. It was as though something in me were being played with a bow. It drew from the vitals of my life and being and plunged me into a voluptuousness that cannot be described.

It was as though invisible hands were touching me and pouring a rich current of electricity through me and into me. My eyes closed, my body relaxed. Like a million hands pressing my body, torturing me with a delicious torture, that sound . . . or was it music? . . . enwrapped me and carried me out of myself into an orgy of physical hysteria.

No, I cannot explain it. I cannot make myself clear.

It was not alone sexual, not alone sensual. It transcended every and all physical pleasure I have ever known. All my body, all my soul and mind and conceptions were thrown into a mael-stromic wave of incomparable joy, of supreme pleasure that was not unlike pain. For ages or minutes I was not capable of thought or action, only of the exquisite drinking of sensation. I felt myself going mad. Then I writhed on the bed, a prisoner of senses and pleasure. Faster and faster and more rich the sound came from the little man's hands, rhythm after rhythm consumed me and lighted fires of passion and madness in me that are unspeakable, unfathomable . . .

Then it stopped.

I was left panting and in pain at the contrast. I was hardly conscious. Every nerve in my body was torn and strained, every muscle exhausted, every fiber of me trembling. I did not see the old man go nor the old woman come in with my robe, and I hardly regained complete understanding of actual life again until I was being led downstairs by Miss B., whose firm arm was tightly around me, guiding me and bracing me for fear that I fall. I tried to speak, to ask questions, but I found no voice. I felt myself being led out to the waiting chair and carried off by our coolies.

Then I fainted completely from exhaustion, and knew noth-ing until I found myself in the ladies' dressing-room of one of the foreign clubs of Shanghai with an Irish attendant holding smelling salts under my nose.

I asked after Lady D. and her friend, when I could talk.

"Lady D.?" queried the girl. "But it was a gentleman brought you here. He said you had a fainting spell and to look after you, Lady. But there was nobody else."

A man? Who? Where had he found me? Where were my English friends? What did it all mean?

I never found out. I have never been able to find the house of the strange Chinese violin. I could not find my two friends in Shanghai again, either to thank them or to learn more of the extraordinary "experience." And before I could ever trace them or the wonderful house of the ivory panels that turns pleasure into madness, I left Shanghai ... quite suddenly and precipitately.

Explanation? None in so far as I know. I have read of strange experiences with vibrations. It is a fact that the Medieval Chinese could kill by breaking the nerve cells of the body with the vibrations of a gong. It is true that at a certain Tabernacle in America, so-called "religious" fanaticism which was really sensual or even sexual, has been produced by a hidden organ pipe which vibrated at a certain pitch which the ear could not detect. But I have never had an explanation for what I shall always remember as my "experience of the Chinese violin."

I said I left Shanghai soon.

The reason is to be found in the handsome but difficult person of Huan Kai. I have said his personality was changing, but I cannot describe the fear he was beginning more and more each day to inspire within me.

In the first place his jealousy became unbearable. Spies were set upon me, even when I walked in the garden with the five little dogs he had bought me. And then, there was something increasingly evil in the huge almond eyes of Huan Kai. He was meditating something, and it was something about me. I could feel that.

I began to recall stories that little Bonny Walke, of questionable veracity, had told me about him. Two wives, both very wealthy, had died shortly after marrying him. He was pressing me to marry him, almost madly. He was also called "Mr. Gold" for no very pleasant reason.

The result of all this thinking was that I decided to escape before I learned about death in China in some way just as vivid and much more personal than the Death of a Thousand Cuts that I had witnessed with Huan Kai.

No, there was no use fooling myself. I was afraid, and I was going to take no chances. I was counted a very wealthy girl in those days, and I could see no reason why the already full money-bags of Huan Kai should be overstuffed with my money, nor why I should be added to the list of his mysterious defuncts.

I decided to take steps.

First I learned from Meh-ki, the old woman who was devoted to me, that Huan Kai was invariably away towards the first of the new moon. Then I told her my plan. To say she was frightened is to understate. She saw knives and blood in every word I spoke. But she loved me, and after protesting that she too was in her master's spy service and that she would certainly be killed if I escaped, she finally agreed to help me and we made arrangements. I won her at last by promising to take her with me and keep her always as my servant.

Meh-ki first found coolies and a chair which it would be safe to use. She procured a silk rope. Then, when everything was ready, we planned to have the chair waiting for us when the moon was high, at a little distance from the house.

I will never forget waiting for the time.

I knew that Huan Kai's men were at my door, and all over the house. I knew that if anyone in the neighborhood should recognize me, they would betray me for fear of punishment from Huan Kai. I wondered if the chair-coolies would be there, and if they were really trustworthy. I was afraid for their honesty, because I had given them money in advance.

But at last it was time. Meh-ki went first down the knotted rope, and I followed her. It was a distance of about 60 feet to the ground, and I will admit that, through sheer fright and nervousness, I several times nearly lost my hold and fell. I imagined that below me I could see the shadows of Huan Kai's men. I imagined that the silk rope was slipping or being cut.

But when I got to the ground and crept breathlessly away from the palace to where the immediate danger was, I felt the return of a certain security which had been missing since the first day when I set my American foot inside that magnificent but frightful Oriental building, and the doors first closed behind me.

The coolies, thank Heaven, were there. They kept their word and had the chair ready for us, and it was not long before we were being swung along the streets of Shanghai by a roundabout way to the foreign concession. There we went to a hotel where I was known but where, I imagined, Huan Kai would not think of looking for me.

I was wrong.

It must have been about four in the morning. I had been sound asleep, with the little old woman curled up on a mat at the end of my room. Suddenly I was awakened.

It was a curious, instinctive sensation which woke me – one

of those which occasionally warn you about something not yet present but already approaching. I stared about me. I could see quite clearly, because of the peculiar lighting system of the hotel which shone over the panel-partitioning from the outer hall. My "room" was really an alcove, and I began to realize that it was senseless to expect security by locking the door, as anyone intent on harm could perfectly well crawl over the wall.

I could see nothing wrong, but I *felt* something. In the dim light, I examined every corner. Nothing. I got out of bed and went for my dressing-gown. Suddenly I changed my mind, threw the dressing-gown on the bed, and fumbled in my handbag for a little pearl-handled revolver given me by my first husband. There was actually not a cartridge in it, but I forgot this in my excitement. I remember how safe I felt as my hand closed on it.

Then suddenly, before I could cross the room again, I knew that there was some one standing just outside the wall, almost directly through the partition from where I was standing. I was paralyzed. I could not have made the slightest move.

There was a slight patting sound outside.

There was the faintest tap or knocking of something on the floor. I could not see from where I was crouching at the foot of the partition, but I knew that some one was peering over the top of that wall.

Then there was a little thud on the bed. The sense of presence faded, and I seemed at once to know that whoever had been up at the partition had gone away. But it was minutes before I dared to relax or to turn my head and look.

Nothing had changed. There was nobody there. Meh-ki's breathing went on rhythmically as she slept. But when I reached to pick up my dressing-robe I saw that a long knife was sticking in it, buried up to the hilt in the folds of its thick, quilted silk, and in the bedding.

Then I realized what had happened. The dressing-gown, thrown on the bed, had looked like somebody lying there in the half light. If I had not had that lucky impulse to get my little revolver ... unloaded and all ... I would have had about ten inches of razor-edged steel, thrown by a hand that would not miss, stuck through my neck where it joins the shoulder. It was an interesting thing to think over.

Well, I admit that there was no more sleep for me that night. I did not want to terrify Meh-ki by waking her and telling her. But I curled up on a mat on the other side of my bed and on the floor where nobody looking could ever have seen me, and there I sat until daylight came and until I was nearly dead with cramp from just squatting there. I decided that I was going to leave Shanghai as early as I could and get as far away from Huan Kai and his knife-throwing servants as possible.

And it was not over yet.

Meh-ki awoke with daylight. She saw me crouching beside the bed and tottered over to me, thinking probably that I was hysterical. She went out to have some tea sent to me, and she never came back. Her body was found at the end of the hall with a long knife through the back of her neck.

The excited house-servants, accompanied by Sikh policemen, brought her to my room about two hours later. They suspected me, until I showed them the hole in the dressing-gown and the bedding, and explained what had happened. They are well-trained men, these imported Sikhs, and they wrote careful notes to make a report of a strange burglar who throws knives at American girls in hotels and kills their servants.

Naturally, I told them that I suspected nobody, and they could make no other report.

I did not wait to go to the Consulate. I just took a train that morning for Hong Kong. I was taking no more chances on Huan Kai.

It is very curious, now that I look back on it, this affair of Huan Kai. I had been afraid of him from the very first instant I saw him at the Hong Kong "dive." Afraid, but drawn to him. I could not ever have loved him, but he fascinated me. What is there about women that is so perverse, so incomprehensible? I wonder if anyone will ever explain it. We love one man because he beats us, and another because he does not. We hate one man who is a cad and we love another who is worse. We spend years on end with a man we are frightened of or whom we despise, pretending to ourselves that we love him, being jealous of him, wanting him, fighting for him, and we are cruel, mean, unfair to another who is sweet and good and loves us, and we will have nothing to do with him.

Personally, I do not like women very much, but they are curious people to watch.

I would not have missed the experience of Huan Kai for all the world. But marry him? Never. Love him? Ridiculous. Admire him? Enjoy him? Well, I'm a woman . . .

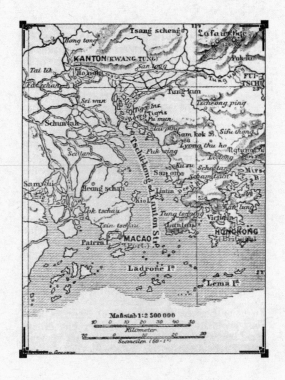

CHAPTER XIX

Map of Hong Kong.

There is not much more to tell about my days in China. There was nothing more exciting about my journey to Hong Kong than the suspicion that mysterious Chinamen were hiding in corners of my railway compartment, to throw knives. It was not a pleasant journey.

Furthermore, I made no attempt to avoid the "European" city of Victoria for the few days I remained there, and I stayed at the stuffiest and most thoroughly Anglo-Saxon hotel I could find and sought the company of the most decent, and safe, and inarticulate of lieutenants of Her Majesty's foreign service.

However, before I left Hong Kong for Java, Borneo and other romantic countries, I got to know more about how the visiting foreigners like myself lived when they did it conventionally. Some little things that happened were funny and some pathetic. I think I would do well to include a few.

For instance, the bazaars.

The effect of the bazaars on the foreign visitor is curious. In the first place one buys all sorts of useless and very pretty things at a price that seems cheap but is really much more than any Chinese person would have to pay. Very often you don't know what the real use or purpose of the thing you buy is, and of course you have no idea what the decorative Chinese writing on it means. You are generally given to understand that these inscriptions are good luck charms or some such thing. And generally they are nothing of the sort.

There was a woman from St. Louis who was making a tour of the world with her newly rich husband. Now in those days it was a fairly reckless thing to go globetrotting. There were none of your round-the-world cruises at low rates that the average family can afford once every five years. To trip round the world meant something, if only a lot of money. And that was just what this woman had. I have forgotten her name, but she was a type that most of us have seen only too often, the kind who, from being a simple daughter of trades-people, had grown into a money-snob. Moreover she was decidedly fat, decidedly nosey, and decidedly overbearing. All this description is necessary for you to appreciate the picture of what happened to her.

I saw her in a Hong Kong bazaar one day. She had two maids with her to carry packages, and she was out to get, I suppose, the largest collection of Chinese bric-à-brac in the Middle West. We followed her a bit, my companion and I, and were amazed at the wholesale way in which she permitted herself to pay money for things which she could have bought for half the price in St. Louis, or at least in any American Chinatown.

At one booth her eagle eye caught sight of a very gaudy type of silk garment which the Chinese make for export purposes only. It was satin and embroidered, thick like embossing, with every conceivable design and color, and right in the center of the top part or jacket, worked into a circle, were two conventionalized Chinese characters. Upon asking what they meant, she was assured by the calm Oriental who sat in the booth that it was "one piece good luckee happiness" or words to that effect.

All would have been well if Mrs. Newlyrich had not been so nosey. A youngish American ... I think he was a missionary ... happened to be at a near-by booth, poring over some Chinese manuscripts. It was easy to see that he could read them and our dear traveling lady called out to him after she had bought her silk garment.

"Do you read this language, young man?" she asked. "If you do, I wish you would tell me what this business on the jacket means. The Chinks say it's good luck, but I'd like to know what kind of good luck."

The young man's nose came out of his reading. He lifted his hat politely and came over to her. He took one look at the symbol which appeared over the front of the jacket, exactly where the good lady's stomach would come, and said very seriously:

"Madam, it may be that he told you it meant good luck but the real meaning of those characters is something like this: stuffed and bursting with over-self-indulgence."

And then he raised his hat once more and calmly returned to his books. My companion and I did not hear what followed. We had to conceal our laughter.

There are hundreds of such anecdotes which one hears – such as the young lady who discovered that the lovely costumes she got to use as lounging jackets were the very special attire of Chinese girls of a very special profession, and the other whose magnificent yellow metal vessel that she got to keep the ferns in in her Middleville home was originally planned for a very different purpose.

I left Hong Kong for the Dutch Indies. I had not gotten over my nervousness about Huan Kai, nor had I satisfied my appetite for the East. I wanted to know more and to see more.

And there was still pulling at me that strange and almost magic power that has always called me away into new places, toward new faces, deeper into the Orient, my book, my mirror of people.

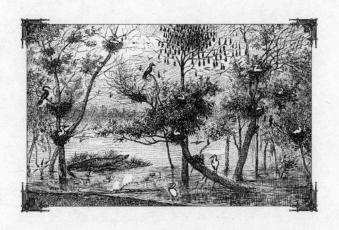

CHAPTER XX

Illustration from *Two Years in the Jungle: The Experiences of a Hunter and Naturalist in India, Ceylon, the Malay Peninsula and Borneo* by William T. Hornday.

This chapter opens in Singapore, winds through Java and plunges me into the heart of Borneo, that fantastic island which legend has famed for a "wild man" who does not exist.

There is no use in dragging out this narrative by following in exact detail my movements and trivial vicissitudes. This is no attempt to write my autobiography, for my life all by itself is no more interesting than anybody else's life. All I want to do is to report some of the more interesting phases of it and to keep you as well as myself from being bored by it. A vicarious pleasure for a woman who is no longer young: a few smiles, a few flashes of those unusual things that might have happened to anybody, but actually happened to me.

So we go to Singapore in a big jump after running away from Huan Kai and Hong Kong, forgetting, if you please, that it is a long way around the peninsula of Indo-China to the Malay states and that in my day you had to do it by boat, and that a boat ride, even in those curious waters, may be a commonplace business. This one was . . . But Singapore deserves a little time and picturing.

I stayed there only long enough to look around and plunged ahead on adventure, but, brief as it was, it was a fascinating sojourn.

Bustle, hustle, rustle, rattle. Singapore was then a cauldron of boiling humanity, of all colors, shapes, sizes, and races. All it needed was the motor-cars of today to rival Paris, New York, or Berlin.

The 'rikishas are faster than in Japan, or so they seemed to me. The little Japanese runners were bewildering enough, but their bigger Malay brothers were more so. Furthermore, they were cheaper. If I remember rightly you could be whirled around that city for something like 25 cents an hour. It was as good as Coney Island.

Singapore is distinctly English, despite the population of about 140,000 Chinese. Like Hong Kong's British capital, Victoria, the European construction was evident even then, for already it had been British for nearly a century.

I remained in the city only long enough to plan the rest of my journey through Java and Sumatra and to engage the necessary passages, but I was lucky enough to make friends who gave me a glimpse of the exotic night-life which rivaled anything I had seen in Paris or elsewhere.

Curious city.

You expect to find the East, and you find only rumor of it. It is as though the whirling 'rikishas, the toiling coolies, the resplendent Chinese merchants and arch-millionaires were sketches hung in an English frame. It is an odd impression. Take Raffles Square, for instance. The *Carrefour* of the Opera at the business hour of the busiest day in a modern year is not as roaring and raging and teeming as was that famous square in that earlier day. Nor is lower Broadway nor Charlottenstrasse.

I had not come for this. I wanted to push on and to leave this sort of thing behind me. Why go to the other side of the world to see the same old things?

I went on to Java in an immaculate Dutch ship whose cleanliness was so extreme as even to make me a little embarrassed. It was an interesting boat because the officers were fine, keen, order-conscious Dutchmen and the crew were Malays. I find there is a vague idea in the minds of those who have never traveled in that part of the world that Malays and other yellow or brown-skinned races do not make good sailors of the European type. Believe me, this is a myth. That crew was masterful, controlled by the Europeans who knew their business and knew how to handle the men. It was impressive to watch them at work.

From Singapore to Tandjong Priok, which is the port of Batavia, we took about 36 hours of travel through the balmiest air and over the bluest water one could imagine. We crossed the Equator at 11 in the evening, and I remember how everyone seemed to stay up and on deck, almost as though they expected to see an actual line. Funny, humans are.

A *djongo*, or "boy" followed me from the port of Batavia in the very up-to-date little train, taking care of me and my baggage as though he were to remain with me through life. They are even better than the "boys" in China. This one was fifty years old.

At Batavia ... and I mean the New City, or Weltetreden and not the Old City where nobody can live but the natives ... I again found a pretty modern place and would have been glad to get away into the interior sooner than I did, but circumstances held me for a while.

In fact, circumstances began right then and there which gave rise to one of the most extraordinary adventures of my life, and I found myself plunged into something that was at least as bad if not worse than my experience with Huan Kai.

My hotel was Dutch, spotless, orderly, comfortable and in general the sort of place one can live in as we do in America or Europe. I spent three weeks in going around that magnificent garden of a city, getting new sensations, new smells of flowers, new food, having my first (and many other) *rijstafel* or rice-table, which compares favorably with the kitchen of any other country in the world, learning to love the native women in their *sarongs* of batik and watching them create these unbelievable works of art.

Then one day I met a man.

Shall I call him the Wild Man of Borneo? It would be amusing to continue that legend, but it has nothing to do with Djoet-ta, Prince of Koetai.

A legend of a totally different sort has even grown up about me in connection with this extraordinary young man. It runs to the effect that I became the "friend" of a Dyak headhunter ... not bad for an American girl, but fairly inaccurate.

Djoet-ta was not a head-hunter in the sense that is ordinarily implied. He was a curious mixture of a very handsome young man, truly Dyak by race, but Europeanized by contact and environment. His father was one of the most brilliant native geniuses on the Island of Borneo, and had had the extraordinary intelligence to leave his wild island and to attend the funeral of Queen Victoria. He knew very little of things European, but he came to England and learned a lot. He made a name for himself while in London, brought respect for himself and his little country to a real state of being, purchased everything that pleased or amused him, and sent it back to furnish his palace with.

But it is not with the father we are concerned, but rather with the Prince himself. He had gone to England with his father, as a very young man, had remained there in a good public school, and had been admitted to one of the crack regiments later on.

Djoet-ta, or "Joe," as English-speaking people called him, had returned to his native land only the year before my visit, bringing with him a yacht which was one of the marvels of the Dutch Indies, three "horseless carriages" (which had no roads to run on), and no end of material that young English gentlemen are supposed to need and have to play with.

The result of all this experience upon a young savage was remarkable, and you can guess for yourself that I was not only amused but very pleased to have made his acquaintance.

Our meeting occurred at the home of the Dutch Resident of Bandoeng who was arranging my papers for me so that I could circulate more freely through the islands. I had scarcely arrived after making the tiresome journey from Batavia by what was called a railroad through a land so fanciful that I had the impression of being rolled through stage scenery. I was very tired and very much disinterested in people. The Resident was as kind as could be, and made me at home in his own house where his charming old wife fussed over me as though I had been her own daughter.

At dinner I sat opposite a curious-looking young man who seemed half afraid of me, and stared at me with the same expression as you can see in the eyes of a wild animal. He was very tall, very solid, not the rich brown color of the usual Malay, but bronze and of sharper features in a way that suggested the American redskin.

I supposed that the reason why the Resident made no

attempt to introduce me was that he spoke only Javanese or some Island language. But there I was wrong.

He had not taken his eyes off me during the whole five minutes that we had been seated at table. Suddenly he spoke and in very good English, too.

"Why did you come to the Indies?" he asked.

He spoke with a strained sort of voice and yet without any inflection. It was an odd voice and an odd question.

The Resident and his wife looked concerned, but said nothing. In fact I had an impression that they had not been at ease all along. But before I could reply to this young man's sudden question the Resident made the introduction he had delayed so long.

"This is Miss Crocker, Your Highness," he said, and, turning to me, "The Prince of Koetai favored us with a visit this evening. He has only recently returned from England."

It was said in a way that made me wonder if he was apologizing for something. Later I learned that the dear old Resident had been afraid I would resent being introduced to a "gentleman of color," and that by some word or gesture I might express my feelings and so precipitate an "international incident" in miniature.

But the Resident was relieved at once. I answered Prince "Joe," as I learned to call him later, and made him a reply that was just as important as his question.

"I came here to meet you," I said.

He took me literally and very seriously.

"But how did you know about me?"

The Resident had to explain in some language I did not understand that I had meant to be humorous. The Prince smiled.

He smiled as a little child will grin. He was very much like a little child who was discovering things everywhere. He was very shy, and did not say anything more at all during the meal. But he kept staring at me as though I were something of which he had never seen the like in his life.

After dinner, he disappeared for a time, and I had coffee with the Resident and his wife and learned something of the story of "Prince Joe." He was a great friend of the Resident and of all the governors, both Dutch and British, throughout the Indies. He traveled about in his yacht with a native crew, and spent about half the year, dressed in European costume, visiting all the officials. The other half he spent in Koetai, his own country on the Island of Borneo, up the Mahakam River. His father was known as the "Wise One" and was the greatest friend of the European dominion, helping to keep relations with the native nations friendly.

Prince Joe came back later, riding a beautiful English horse and leading another.

Would I like to ride? I would, but was not dressed for it. Why did I not dress, then? Simple: like that. He looked at everything directly and saw no reason why things should not be as he wanted them. I was amused. Well, children have their way, and this huge child, half savage, half public-school boy, had his, for I put on some riding things from my luggage and went off with him into the rich flora of Java.

It was one of the queerest evenings I have ever spent.

It was almost without conversation. We simply rode our horses and looked at each other. And it was very pleasant too. This young man really interested me, as much by his strange quiet manner as by a wildness that seemed to be in him. It was something that I could not explain very well, for although he was nearly a savage by birth and early environment, yet he was quite conventional, quite like a very tanned young Englishman. And yet, he was not . . .

There was something about his eyes. It was most of all noticeable when we had gotten away from the town and into the rich country, reeking with perfume and the smell of the earth. They seemed to light up, as though fires were burning far back inside of him. He said almost nothing, but he looked at me. Constantly.

When it grew really darkish, we went back to the Residence, and Prince Joe said good-night to me, timidly, but in the best English manner.

Next day the Resident's wife talked to me about Prince Joe. She was really pleased that I had not taken the haughty attitude that most white visitors take towards the natives of the Indies. She told me that the poor young man really suffered because he had lost favor with his own people, having grown more or less European, and on the other hand he felt that he did not belong to the white people he had learned to imitate and to like. Most Americans would do well to put themselves in the place of the negroes to whom they affect to be so superior.

I didn't see Prince Joe all the next day, but I amused myself by walking about Bandoeng, watching the natives and lazing in the miraculous Javanese climate and landscape.

After dinner, I made up my things ready to leave in the morning, for my papers had all been arranged, and went out into the cool air for a little walk before retiring. It was delicious. All about me were new things, new shapes of trees, new little animals, monkeys chattering, fluttering things, creeping things, friendly things. Bandoeng is not cut into a jungle but touches the water on one side and a fairly dense forest mingles with the town on the other. I had not the slightest fear. The natives are docile and sweet. There are no savage beasts. There was just an ancient fairyland, laden with the perfume of the East. I was in a reverie, utterly happy.

Suddenly, from nowhere at all, appeared four human shapes, indistinct in the dark. Words were spoken in some language. One of them stepped towards me and held his hands out straight towards me, the palms down. I did nothing, could do nothing, not even step back. Then one gave a sharp word of command, and they all stepped to me and laid their hands on me, not roughly, and led me along with them.

You will wonder why I did not scream or resist. Aside from the fact that it would have been useless, since Bandoeng was too far away for anyone to hear, I was perfectly paralyzed. The suddenness, the unexpectedness of it, left me incapable of any thought or action. I simply walked along.

I could not even see my captors clearly in the darkness, but I was able to observe that they did not wear the *sarong* of the Javanese, and seemed to be naked, or nearly so. We went deep into the wood, I stumbled over the underbrush, and the puttees of my riding habit – which I had decided to adopt as a regular costume – kept catching on twigs and long grass.

Then they stopped, and the one who had held out his hands to me did so again. Then he reached out and lifted me off the ground as though I were a mere doll, and strode forward with me while the others vanished.

It was now that I began to be afraid. I felt myself power-less in the arms of this man. I felt myself alone in a forest with nobody to turn to, nobody to notice before morning that I had gone. I was just a young girl and I was very frightened and I wanted San Francisco and all the things I had been running away from very much indeed.

Then I saw that we were on the banks of a small river, and that the other natives were there in a little black group. The man who carried me stepped down to the edge, and I could see a long boat with outriggers on one side, moored there. He stepped right in with me and deposited me without ceremony on the bottom, and the others pushed off after getting in also, and we were sliding through the forest before I could realize it.

Eerie lights filtered down through the trees. Monkeys in families or tribes were swinging in the branches and screaming. The sound of soft paddles mingled with those of the forest, while I sat there, huddled and trembling.

In twenty minutes we broke out of the wood and the air became suddenly salty, and in a few moments more I saw nothing more about me but water, and knew, from the behavior of the canoe, that we were either at sea or in a bay of some kind.

Nothing but silence and the paddles. My abductors had scarcely uttered a word since first I set eyes on them.

A seabird cawed overhead, unseen.

I was very chilly from the cold, and numb with fright. And then, seemingly quite near, I saw a light, and behind the light, dimly appearing, the form of a ship. The men paddled straight for it, driving the boat hard. It was further away than it seemed, and it took us over five minutes to get alongside. I was more bewildered still when I realized that, instead of being a junk or some native boat, it was a modern yacht that might have been built in Glasgow or Havre or New Bedford.

Then, while the leader of the four men was drawing us close to the ship by a line which dangled from the stern, the real truth dawned on me.

Prince Joe!

Was it possible, or was it merely an absurd idea?

I had little time to reflect, however, for we crawled along the hull to the port side, and the head man pointed to a rope ladder which I knew better than to refuse to climb. Up I went, about three feet to the gunwales of the yacht. Other scantily clad natives clustered around and stared at me. But no one touched me. I began to lose my fear.

When the head man came over the side, he led me to a gangway and I followed him down below. There was not much headroom, but I could stand comfortably below decks, and at last there was some light. I could see that my captors were no Javanese, but much taller, much more rugged than the sleek islanders I had seen.

I had scarcely time to look about me, when another voice spoke sharply and the head man vanished. I was left alone in a cramped little cabin, the furnishings executed in leather and mahogany, and I dropped into a seat.

Then the door opened, and a voice that I recognized said:

"I'm very sorry."

It was Prince Joe.

He was dressed in a garment that resembled the Javanese *sarong*, but was made of woven silk rather than of batik material. There was something like a turban on his head, and he looked for all the world like a person playing at charades.

He stood there and stared at me as he always had, timid and faun-like.

"I didn't know how else to do it," he explained. "You would never have come by yourself, and I want you to visit my country with me."

What was I to say? It was like talking to a young boy. There was no use getting angry, no sense in saying "How dare you?"

What I said was:

"You didn't ask me."

He just looked and smiled.

"You'll come?"

"And if I say 'No'?"

"I will send you back at once."

"What about the Resident?"

"He will be very angry."

"How will you explain?"

"Will you write him a note? Please tell him you wanted to come. I will have it taken to him."

He was pleading. I could see that he was very excited. Then it occurred to me that this half-savage boy was in love with me, that he was more frightened of my refusal than he was of the whole Dutch Government and all the complications which could arise out of this absurd abduction. He was in love with me, and it was not the cheap, sentimental thing that civilized people know, but instead it was like a great, muscular, wild puppy wanting his master to be kind to him.

I wrote the note.

I said that I had met the Prince and had decided to see Borneo with him as my guide. I wondered what the formal old Resident would say and think, and what crime I was committing by going away unprotected by my papers. I didn't even care that all my clothes and other things were in Bandoeng in my trunks, and that I had nothing save what was on my body at the moment.

But what a lark! Captured by savages, abducted by a Dyak prince, carried away into the wilds of Borneo by the Wild Man himself! What an adventure!

Well, it turned out to be even more of an adventure than I had bargained for.

I was rather a willing "prisoner." I was given a sweet little cabin to myself on this fantastically modern mahogany yacht by its owner, just as fantastically a combination of a jungle chieftain and a Guardsman. I was treated with the utmost respect. I was mooned at and followed about the little ship by a human "doggy" hoping for a master. I was talked to in very civil monosyllables and made to feel that I had somehow taken advantage of a child.

And, believe me, I had.

We set out across Macassar Strait, which separates Java from the island of Borneo, and for one day and two nights I was blown upon by all the cinnamon-laden winds of the Indian Ocean, filled full of a rich delight in living and the pleased sense that a young girl has when she is being pleasantly naughty. And that savage royal child, Prince Joe, gone perhaps a little mad as he carried me away into the heart of his country, was so sweet, so simple and happy and infantile and kind, that I will always look back upon those hours as some of the fairest and most peaceful in my life.

We sailed for Balik-Papan first, which I understand is now a petroleum depot, and I was fascinated by two things: first, the antics of the native dockworkers, who were loading and unloading everything you can think of, particularly some brown hogs who had lost their squeal because they were packed in wicker cylinders so tight they could not move nor squirm and were piled up like logs; and secondly at the dignity of the Dutch officials who came aboard. These were efficient gentlemen, and although they said nothing about my missing papers because of the power and authority of my young host, I could see they were puzzled and not a little annoyed.

I wondered what the San Francisco press would have given to have my "latest story." I had not forgotten their special attention to me when I was in Hawaii. "Aimée and the Wild Man of Borneo" would have made a good headline for the Sunday supplements.

We tarried only a short time in Balik-Papan, leaving at noon and reaching Samarinda in the early evening.

It was the most astonishing journey. We steamed up the Mahakan River inland to the very heart of Borneo, through a dense jungle, while monkeys screamed in the trees overhead, crocodiles splashed about us or lay like imitation logs on the banks of the river, and birds of bewildering plumage fluttered and cawed over and around the ship, and the purr of our gasoline engine mingled oddly with the inexplicable sounds of the jungle.

Whatever curious qualities Prince Joe may have had, there was one thing about him that was remarkable for native intelligence and modern European knowledge and skill and that was his handling of the yacht *Palipoeti*. He never left the wheel, and he steered her round shallows, avoiding rocks, following the deep water at whichever side of the large, dangerous, shallow river it might be, and slid her gracefully through the water-lilies and algae that sometimes caused trouble and even wrecks, so I was told.

During this run, he was less attentive to me, and I had time to lounge by myself in a deck-chair and admire the green passing show. Sometimes we would pass settlements, native clusters of thatched huts built high and narrow on stilts in the river itself, with carved and painted walls. He would occasionally stop and anchor the boat while a tribal chief and his painted crew would paddle out to us and carry on a rhythmic, monotonous conversation in their own language, and then would paddle back.

Prince Joe had changed his costume from the first moment we reached the shores of Borneo and was wearing the silk *sarong* of his race. But when we steered into the jungle regions that flank the Mahakan River, he came to me and made excuses for the fact that he would have to change into something far simpler in order not to disturb the sense of proportion of the island natives, who had no faith in the customs of civilization.

"Simpler" his costume certainly became. It consisted of a loin-cloth and a straw-like girdle with a fringe. But his body, standing there at the wheel, bronze and perfect in youthful power, muscled and rippling with every little movement, was really divine. A European or an American would have been conscious of such a body, but not he. He was only vaguely aware of the European proprieties, and soon made no restrictions of his movements or his contacts with me. And as the sun slowly dropped behind the Nippa-palms that lived in and caressed the water, I saw this young god, shining in the glow of the golden light, a bronze Achilles, something aflame.

Yes, I liked him.

We reached the last government post at Long Iram, and again I was embarrassed by the searching looks the Resident gave me when my "visit" was explained to him by the Prince. But my luck held, and his power likewise.

Pushing on up the river, we plunged deeper and deeper into the jungle. The character of the country changed, and also that of the people. They were a different race from the Malays of the coast towns. The cheek-bones were more prominent, the skin a lighter brown. They were Dyaks, head-hunters, men of a jungle wilderness like my prince.

We arrived. We arrived at Tenggorong where the magnificent palace of Prince Joe stood, the seat of the native government of Koetai. It is hard to describe it, not only because my memory has grown dim, but because it was so surprisingly in contrast with anything I had expected.

Swarms of natives poured to the river's edge to greet their wandering prince. Bearers brought a magnificent Sedan-chair to receive their royalty. I was installed beside him. Priests, or medicine men, or whatever they were called, in grotesque masks, beat upon skins stretched over gourds and others played on weird wood and string instruments.

Then the palace.

It was about 1000 feet square, of exquisitely carved wood, and removed from the river by about half a mile. The upper part was painted gray in good European paint, while the lower part or paneling which bore the carvings was dyed in soft, beautiful colors with native herb-dye. It was fronted by a verandah about 100 or more feet long and very deep, and leading up to this platform were white marble steps.

It came upon me that I was being treated as a sort of goddess or living spirit, and I tried to find out from Prince Joe what it was all about, but he looked blankly at me and said nothing.

Later I observed that he never attempted to explain nor even to cope with the two fundamentally different parts of his life and training. He accepted simply, as a child, what happened. It pleased him childishly to bewilder and alarm his subjects a little by some of the "miracles" which he had brought from England, but he never tried to change them, nor to explain. I often wondered how much he understood himself and how much he accepted from mere habit.

Then I met his father.

He was known, in his native language which I dare not try to imitate in phonetics, as the "Wise One." He was an extraordinary man. Tall ... about six-foot-three ... bearded like the Prince Edward he had met on his Great Adventure abroad, bronze, and clad in a *sarong* over which he wore a British officer's belt and a British saber. He was easily discerned as a born ruler. He spoke English very little, but was able to shake my hand and to say:

"How do you do thank you if you please," so that I knew what he meant.

Then began three weeks of astounding life. There is little use and less space for me to go into the details of it, but it consisted of fishing, hunting with the much-described poison arrows and blowguns (not that I used them), paddling through the tiny tributaries to the great river, and romancing in the moist, rugged jungle of Borneo with a prince who became inarticulate half the day and much too articulate the rest of the time.

But trouble came.

This trouble makes a good story. There was no doubt that Prince Joe was growing more and more in love with me. I do not write this with any conceit nor with any sense of boasting.

He was a strange child of the islands and had been spoiled curiously by an exposure to the civilization which was too much for him to swallow all at once. He came back to his native country with a sense of having lost something, much as he had known nostalgia for his Borneo when in England.

Then I came into the picture. I was the symbol of all he had lost, all the new things he had learned to admire and to wonder at. It was natural that I should seem to him something far more valuable than I really was. At any rate, in love he was, and that was the cause of it all.

"It" became noticeable one day when the prince and I returned from a picnic. We had taken a basket of food, American fashion, and had rambled over the most extraordinary country, and I had learned the names of dozens of birds, of plants, of so many things . . . all of which I, of course, promptly forgot.

As our canoe came silently to the river landing where a very plausible road led up to the palace, there was a little knot of Dyak men pow-wowing in a group, all of them very much painted as to the face with earth or clay and seeming very excited.

Joe's face became suddenly animal. There was fear in it. There was suspicion. Paddling, kneeling in the bow, as is the queer habit in that country, he motioned me to be still. Every sign of the European in him disappeared. He was immediately an alert, wild head hunter of the island of Borneo.

I obeyed him. Unspoken force compelled me to slide to the bottom of the canoe, and I was frightened of something I could neither see nor understand.

Instead of going straight to the mooring, Prince Joe gave a vigorous thrust and sent us whirling out into the middle of the river where a strong current took us like mad over to the other side. I felt it pull us. I could see nothing but the sky from my position. But I felt a slight tap on the bottom of the canoe, and glanced down my nose almost unconsciously. There lay a tiny arrow as though it had fallen from the clouds.

Some one in that knot of men on the shore had favored me with his blowgun, aiming it high in the air, and letting the dart describe a wide arc. I had seen it done with an uncanny precision. I knew that the point contained a poison as sure as cyanide.

Amusing contemplation.

Out of sight and out of shot, the prince relaxed.

"What does it mean?" I asked.

He became the English schoolboy again.

"They are only savages. They do not understand you. They do not love you." He was apologizing for them as a missionary might have done. It would have been amusing, had it not been tragic.

"What have I done?" I asked, and I pointed out that I had already been at the palace for over two weeks and that they had not seemed to object to me until now.

"It is my father," he said. "When I inherit, he knows that you will be my queen. He wishes me to take a native queen, but that I will never do."

Complicated!

He had never before mentioned to me that I was to "be his queen," and certainly I had never consented to such a proposal. I told him so. The information made very little impression.

"You will be my queen," he insisted, "because you cannot leave Koetai without me. You have been happy, have you not? Why should you not stay?"

There was no time to argue. I passed it over. I asked what we were to do next.

The wild man appeared in his eyes again. For answer he whirled the dugout in the river and drove it across to the other side once more. We followed the bank in silence until we came to a little stream. We pushed through water-lilies and branches that overhung the stream and made our way slowly up. After half a mile or so we could go no further. He motioned me to follow him and we dragged the canoe into some bushes on the bank and started forcing our way through the heavy, jungle undergrowth.

Joe was a picture. Every muscle and nerve in his lithe body was taut. Like a panther he crept ahead of me, and never have I been so conscious of the natural clumsiness of the civilized person as I was then.

We came to a clearing, and I could see the palace less than a hundred yards away. We reached the picket fence that surrounded the castle and crawled under a washed-out place and found ourselves inside, unhurt, but very nervous.

I retreated at once to my "passang grahan," or guesthouse, in the palace enclosure. I made hysterical and undefined plans for leaving. I had had enough. Then I suddenly heard a weird, strange piping. It was a mad reed, an insane flute playing about half a mile away. At first it disturbed me only by its weirdness, until it came upon me that its meaning was even more terrible than its sound.

It was the "Kanjor Dodo," the flute of the head-dance. It meant that the entire tribe would be inflamed into a state of fanaticism by the dance of death ... that only a human head could satisfy the religious lust which the flute was fanning.

I have learned later that the Dutch and the British have forbidden the playing of the "Kanjor Dodo" in the island as the most direct means of suppressing the head-hunting of the natives. But in the days of my visit to Borneo no such suppression existed. Why was it playing? What did it mean? I could only imagine that it had something to do with the dark hinting Prince Joe had done when we were escaping from the evil-intentioned group by the landing.

Then Joe came running to my "passang," animal again, and out of breath with excitement.

"Come," he said sharply, "I will take you away. It is too late to escape them. That is the war dance. Do you hear the flute?"

I was in a predicament.

"Let me talk to your father," I said. "Let me explain. He will not dare to do me any harm. He will send me away peacefully. I don't want to stay here."

"Too late. He has already dressed in his ceremonial robes, and the bill of the 'toekang' bird is hanging in his ears. The entire country is alarmed. It is the 'takvet pared,' the fear of weakness, that you have inspired in them. They are afraid that you, a white woman, may be queen, and they will kill us both if they cannot kill you separately. My father has stirred them up in order to make me afraid for you, and now it is too late."

I begged Joe to return and ask him once more to put me aboard the *Palipoeti* and send me back to Long Iram. He finally agreed, and left unwillingly.

It was quite dusk now, and I was growing hysterical. I had to escape ... alone. I ran out of my little house, across the enclosure to the fence through which we had come. I followed, as best I could, the tiny trail we had made from the river. I grew more and more frightened as dark came on. Finally, I started to crawl, never realizing in my fear that in order to see me one would have to be within a few yards, and after half an hour or more of torture I reached the bank of the Mahakan River, torn and scratched up and exhausted.

It took me another hysterical quarter of an hour to find the canoe where he had dragged it. But I cannot describe how happy I felt and how safe when I succeeded in pushing that heavy and unwieldy boat into the current and was caught hold of by the swift waters and whirled out into mid-stream.

It was night, and I could see nothing. I thought of crocodiles, animals that scream overhead and around the banks of the river, monkeys, and creatures that never existed in Borneo. I was in terror of everything, and especially of the lithe, powerful, bronzed, hairless men who were probably behind me in their swifter boats, fanatically pursuing me to carry my head triumphantly back for "the good of the race."

Finally I could stand it no more. I fell asleep with my arm dragging overside, paddle and all. I awoke hours later, cold and wet and sick. I abandoned myself to everything, letting the current take the boat on, drifting and sleeping. I had lost one paddle.

Finally it was morning. The dugout had caught on a low-hanging tree branch and was broadside to it, and the water was nearly mounting over the gunwales.

My fear returned, although I was now so stiff with muscular pain and cold that I thought death was almost better. I pushed clear and began paddling again. I could see a little settlement of Dyak houses with their thatched roofs, and about them children running. I was not seen yet. Could I get by them? You can imagine my terror.

On down the river. All day long I drifted or paddled, half starved, and baked by the sun when I was in the open or bitten by the jungle damp when the river narrowed and flowed through the dank wood country. Then I saw twenty or more canoes ahead of me, and some heavier craft. Round the bend there seemed to be some sort of a larger settlement. I wondered whether I should go boldly by it, or try to hide.

But the stiff current of the river decided for me. I was too weak to paddle against it broadside to land on one bank or the other. I let myself be carried into the bay-like bend ... and found myself at Long Iram. A good stone house stood plainly in sight, proving that I had escaped from the Dyak country, and was at last in the presence of Dutch law and order.

Canoes full of brown Malays looked wonderingly at me. They saw a lone woman in a Dyak canoe who had come drifting down from anywhere. Some chattered at me, pointing towards the stone house on the shore. But I needed no suggestion. I let the current pull me as near to the bank as I could, and brought my dugout up to a little pier. Without even trying to draw it up or take it from the water, I left it behind me and saw it slowly float away and wash downstream, while I staggered up the little hill to the European-built house.

Well, it was a haven. It was a sanctuary. It was, actually, the seat of the most remote Dutch outpost in Borneo.

Captain van B., a fine hearty old soldier of the Dutch Foreign Legion, probably had the surprise of his life when he was called to the door by his pop-eyed little Malay servant, and found a bedraggled, blonde female standing dripping before him.

He exclaimed in Dutch, and I replied in rather breathless English, and he was yet more confused. He had a very limited

English vocabulary, but he brought me inside the house and used practically all of it on me within the next five minutes.

I told him the whole story and the real truth of it. I repeated it so often that he actually understood it and was decidedly shocked. I also had the distinct impression that he was worried, for he sent the little servant out in a hurry and it was not long before a colonial policeman in khaki came in.

Then Captain van B. sent me to bed – which was precisely what I needed – I did not learn for three days what his worry was about. In fact, I remember almost nothing of those three days, although I am told that I was awake part of the time and that I took nourishment, and it was several weeks before the details of my escapade in evading Koetai's jealous tribesmen became clear in my mind.

I was pretty well exhausted, and it was apparently that which caused all the worry. Captain van B. wanted to pack me off in his own steam launch before anything could happen. As it was, I remained some time at Long Iram, trying to recover enough strength to make travel possible. When finally I did get away (under a four-man guard in the fastest boat on the Mahakan River, if you please) there was a wholesome relief in the captain's eyes, and I think I can truly say that I have seldom felt myself so unwelcome.

Although far more docile than the neighboring states, and much more than their kin on the British coast of Borneo, there had always been a certain restlessness on the part of the natives of Koetai. It had long been feared that only a spark was needed to unleash them from their King's dominion and to plunge them into real trouble.

And here I had gone and done it.

You can believe me, then, when I say that Captain van B. was happy to see the last of me, and there was a real tenderness in his manner as he saw me go on board for my trip down the river. Prince Joe came steaming down in the big yacht, quite as worried as the captain, but he learned that none of the natives had pursued me that far. And Captain van B. used some very persuasive method to prevent that young man from hotly pursuing me to make me his princess and future queen. What it was I do not know, but anyway it worked.

One or two more things about Borneo, before I leave, which I did very immediately. The food, for instance, is interesting. The *rijstafel*, especially, which you can get in Paris or Amsterdam or other European places that purport to have Javanese restaurants has little in common with the real dish. In Java, and in Borneo, too, the fruits are the real delicacies. There is the famous "hairy fruit" or *rambutan* whose outside is covered with thick red fibry hairs and contains a delicious seed that looks like a little white piece of garlic. There is the *nassi-tini*, another dish native to both islands which makes you think of our riced chicken, but is infinitely better. And one of the best foods in the whole world ... and I have eaten of many different *cuisines* ... is a thing called *mata-sapi* which is really a fried egg dish that is impossible to describe except by using too many superlatives.

My description of the Dyaks has been rather thin.

I ought to have told you that they are distinguishable from any other of the East Indian races chiefly because they are consistently shaven or even plucked. Hair is considered by them as a shame, and they pluck the eyebrows and lashes of their children at an early age, with the result that all the Dyaks have a peculiar, vacant look about them.

The Islanders are all betel-chewers, and the Dyaks especially. It is a horrible habit, not from the moral viewpoint, for I am not interested in morals, but because all the Dyak women I saw were terribly disfigured by betel. Their lips were swollen and distended and their mouths and teeth stained a dirty brown-red, like dried blood. Some of the girls would otherwise have been very pretty. As a race, they were lithe and well made.

My Prince was fortunate. The "Wise One," his ruling father, had brought him up in the image of the Europeans he had seen on his long-ago trip, and he had neither been plucked nor taught to chew the betel. Otherwise, you can imagine I should never have been interested to the point of having such an absurd adventure.

The Dyaks might be worth writing a book about, if one were learned. They have no real religious cult, a rare thing among savages of any kind. I mean that they have no shrines, no idols, nothing to worship, although they are surrounded by the Malays who are invariably Mohammedan. But they have a conception of metaphysics. They have two souls, according to their own belief. One is called Luva, and makes the body move and function, while the other is called Bruva and does the thinking and yearning and the more abstract things.

The great motive force is the fear of growing weak, the *takvet-pared*. They are a race of athletes, and their lives are consecrated to strength and prowess. A champion of anything – fishing, running, wrestling, jumping, hunting with the blow-pipe – becomes a hero in his local *kampong*, or settlement. He is idolized, and is almost a god, until the next champion arrives.

And they are moral. Moral in the purest sense of the word. It is stated by the people of Borneo that they never lie. Perhaps it is because they are too childlike. Top-spinning is a pastime in Borneo that carries on long after childhood. They make huge tops of their own which will spin for over half an hour and will hum a rich, flute-like note so loud that it can be heard for a mile.

Then there is the more civilized part of the Indies which also has curious customs. There are curiosities, for instance, at Batavia, where I eventually arrived, and where the Resident treated me like a naughty girl and his wife wept on my neck. One of the curiosities is called a "Dutch wife." It may or may not be a sad reflection on the good Dutch women, but it certainly shares your bed. The "Dutch wife" is met with in hotels. You find one in every bed. It is a heavy, round bolster-like affair which lies in the bed with you, and its purpose is to keep you cool.

Last, but not least, let me mention that all the East Indies have one bad habit in common. It is the earthquake habit, and it is decidedly unpleasant.

Riding across Java in a train you can see the craters of I do not know how many volcanoes, and at night they are picturesque and eerie. But those sudden upheavals under the soil of Java are no fun. I did not experience a serious earthquake, but I have been thrown to the ground by a tremor, picked myself up, and been thrown down again by another. This happened to me right in the streets of the new city of Batavia, and I felt very embarrassed. Others were in the same plight, although I saw nobody come so near to having a horse fall on him as I did.

CHAPTER XXI

Snake charmers and jugglers in Bombay in India, *c*. early 1900s.

Now I put all these things behind me. They are only temporary and partial. It was the East I sought, the East I felt, the East I wanted to absorb and breathe and know. And all this China, this Japan, this Malay Coast, this Java and Borneo, were only introductory.

Of course I knew nothing of this. I believed, each time I entered upon a new scene and plunged into a new civilization among a new people, that I had found this mighty East that had been drawing me. But once there, once mixing among these temporary things, I became conscious of a lack of permanence, of a compromise. It was not articulate, it was not clear, but I knew it and felt it.

The loadstone was still drawing me on after I left the Dutch Indies. My small but persistent common sense called on me in its small voice and told me to return to America and accept the compromise that the rich, solid, old Californian life, safe and sure, was offering me.

But one seldom listens to that whisper of common sense.

So, escaping from Borneo, flying away from Java, running from badly handled and ill-conceived adventures, I was drawn towards the source, the spring from whence came all that mystery that I had left my commonplace existence to find. And on the day when the *Parramatta*, a little 5,000-ton steamer of an Oriental line, was warped into the dock at Bombay, I knew that the quest had ended.

You can say, if you choose, that India is British. I yield the point. But India's soul will never concede anything to the Anglo-Saxon system nor to the Nordic philosophy. You can send your missionaries, your lawgivers, your officers; you can build your Yacht Clubs at Bombay where even the highest caste Brahmans cannot enter; you can scorn and dominate (by military) and try to rule some 300,000,000 people, but you can never dominate a country whose composite mind thinks in millenniums, whose ideals have nothing in common with yours, whose age-old civilization goes on believing in the reunion of the Individual with the Supreme Soul.

India. Here I am. A country whose individual life covers over 4,000 years, and whose living breath had been blowing upon me across broad seas, whose fingers had been beckoning me.

The *Parramatta* passed the lighthouse at Colaba Point into the strange double city on two bays. I can hardly recall the picture – I was so impatient to take this vast country into my arms and inhale its amber-flavored breath. I had a vague, haze-dimmed recollection of Hindus, Gujerati, Mahratta, Sikh, Parsee and hundreds of other racial faces and costumes, carts drawn by sleepy oxen, teams, buggies, tramways, victorias, palanquins and good old English coaches, whirling and mingling like a colorful human cocktail. I had not a friend nor an acquaintance in the entire peninsula, excepting Mr. Thos. Cook and his Sons, and to them I trusted myself until I should be able to formulate some plans.

It was just as well, I discovered.

For India, even with the British touch about her cities,

presents a problem of knowing which no other Eastern country can offer by comparison. I do not yet know why.

Picture me in a rich, up-to-date, European hotel. Picture me, trying to free myself of this fear which made me cling to the things I knew and understood, and to throw myself instead into those other things I had come to find.

It was not easy. I needed help. And I found help in an unusual way, a way which was to give me another curious experience and ... I was about to say "get me into trouble." But that we will see later.

The "help" appeared on the day that I visited the American Consulate in Bombay. He was being carried on a litter, or perhaps I should say on an enormous square canopied divan upon which he sat in state and gorgeousness, while a dozen or so soldiers in magnificent costumes bore him stolidly along.

I was in the act of descending the steps of the Consulate. I stopped halfway down to gaze in bewilderment and admiration at the splendor of what I saw ... the train of a Hindu Rajah in full regalia. You have seen it in the cinema ... made in Hollywood, doubtless, but seldom is it given to a Westerner to witness a procession of one of these potentates and their retinue silhouetted against a background of their own native sky.

Anyway, there I stood gaping. And the Rajah saw me, lifted his head a little, drew the cigarette away from his lips, and winked. I said it. He winked.

Well, I suppose if you were to have spent half your life in Northern Canada among the Eskimos, knew their language and habits intimately, and then were to see one standing on a church step, staring bewildered at you in Hohokus, New Jersey ... well, you might be tempted to wink, too.

That is what affected this Rajah. He winked and he smiled, and it was utterly impossible for me not to smile in return. His train passed on, a multicolored crowd following them, the Rajah erect upon his silken cushions, his legs crossed under him, smoking with dignity. It was just a moment. Just a scene from the motion pictures. He was, I supposed, passing on . . . out of my life.

But as I wandered, rather in a trance, down towards my hotel, I was conscious suddenly of some one walking rapidly behind me. Then I felt a slight touch on my shoulder, and a soft, low male voice said:

"If the Memsahib would pause . . ."

I paused. I looked into the eyes of a turbaned bearded soldier of melodramatic appearance. He towered over me, in his white, loose garments, his hand resting upon the handle of a silver-mounted carved dagger, and then he bowed low before me.

"If the Memsahib will accept the compliments of my Master, the Rajah of Shikapur, I, Poonga, am instructed to say that his house and his race will be honored above the stars."

He was holding something out to me. It looked like a tiny packet of silk, and my curiosity overwhelmed any hesitancy I might have had, although I was still unable to reply. I mumbled something of no consequence and allowed the soldier to place this packet in my hands. I stood there staring at it. My swarthy giant spoke again:

"If the Memsahib will permit . . . Poonga will return to his Master with a reply favorable to the question."

All this was in beautifully pronounced English. I was brought out of my trance. I found the fastening cord of the little silk affair, and when I had removed the covering, a crisp piece of pasteboard about two inches wide and rolled into a cylinder was revealed. There was also something hard and heavy rattling inside the tube.

I unrolled it. There fell into my hand a pearl, an absolutely perfect pearl not less than half an inch in diameter, and as lustrous as nacre. The white pasteboard turned out to be a very European visiting-card, across which was written, in pinched characters:

"Please forgive the stupid unconventionality of this, but a new face on the Consulate steps is such a delight and especially when its owner wears a pearl clasp whose beauty and value can be seen at a distance of thirty feet. I am receiving a few persons this evening at my hotel, and it would be a pleasure if you could be among them. My man Poonga will bring you in a litter. Something in your face made me feel that you would not think me a barbarian. Shikapur."

Now here was a case! My pearl clasp which I had all but forgotten had started something. I had purchased it for a considerable sum in Java ... a raw, unpolished pearl, and I had had it mounted to please my own imagination. It turned out to be a beauty, and it seemed now to be acquiring a legend.

Poonga stood erect and obviously waiting for me to say something. Does one accept the invitations of Hindu Rajahs from some unknown territory in the British city of Bombay? I don't know. But I did it.

"Please thank your master," I said to the soldier, "and tell him that I accept with pleasure. My hotel is the V——"

Poonga bowed again, and vanished. One thing struck me as odd. No mention of the enclosed pearl had been made in the Rajah's note.

Nine o'clock.

A porter announced, "Some one to see you, Madam." He sounded as though he were not quite proud of the "Some One," as though he felt a little superior to any one who would have that kind of a "some one" coming to call. I descended, and there was Poonga, dressed in a resplendent silken costume, sword in place and turban new and clean and white, shining above his silken glory like a full moon. Nor was he alone, for behind him a battery of five or six servants waited in a manner nearly military.

He saluted with his back-breaking bow, and gestured me to the door where stood the same magnificent litter upon which I had seen his Master.

Now it is one thing to sit upon such a dais in the Hindu costume, but quite another for an American woman in her evening gown and wrap to assume the cross-legged position which such a device demands. I found myself embarrassed. However, I managed to adjust myself to the situation without too much loss of dignity.

I was lifted and carried in state, the curtains or canopies were dropped and I was as secluded as though I were *purdah* with my veil and headwrap, like the most discreet of Brahman young women.

I scarcely saw where we were going, although I did peek out of the curtains discreetly once, only to be cautioned by Poonga.

"It is not advisable," he whispered, appearing from somewhere beside the litter. "The Memsahib should not reveal to those who do not know and who may not understand that she – not being of my race – is traveling in the chair of my Master."

I understood. I returned to the mystery of the interior.

Then we arrived. It turned out to be not a "hotel," in the usual sense, but a "hotel particulier," in the French meaning of the word, that is to say a private house of really splendid order. I was completely unnerved at the moment of entering that palace, but I did notice that it was of a luxury and magnificence quite commensurate with the glory of an Indian prince.

I was led into a vast hall and then through a corridor of marble, and finally came into a tremendous room where many persons stood or sat or walked about. In English an attendant announced my name. There were other English and Europeans present.

And then, my Rajah detached himself from a group of talkers and came forward to greet me.

His greeting was charming, and his presentation to the celebrities, British, German, French and Hindu, was noble, but suddenly his face darkened as he stared at me, and with very little ceremony he left me standing almost alone.

I was puzzled.

A somewhat painted but well-preserved Englishwoman of certain age who had noticed the sudden change, came over to me.

"What did you say to him, my dear?" she asked. "Did you refuse him something? That is the look he wears when you say 'no.' Nasty temper, you see."

I did not like her. I did not like any of the people. They seemed . . . how shall I say it? . . . a little unreal, a little *wanting*.

Then I wondered. Was it the pearl? Had I forgotten to wear or even to bring his pearl? Was it something significant in India? I did not know. I was rather alarmed, for no definite reason.

There was music, and that then new invention, cocktails, and whisky for the officers. I retreated to one side of the great room and seated myself, very ill at ease, on a low divan and watched the people. I felt "let down." I had expected . . . Heaven knows what, but not this.

Then a voice spoke to me. It was a soft, cultured voice.

"Tired?" it said. "Or just bored?"

I looked up. A tall young Hindu, in European clothes but wearing a turban, was standing beside my divan. He was unusually handsome for a man of any race, and he had a haughtiness in his features that commanded both attention and respect.

"Just a little out of place, I'm afraid," I said. "Your ways are all new to me. I'm just a tourist in your country."

"Tourist?" He seemed genuinely astonished. "But then how did you get here? Forgive my curiosity, but it isn't usual, you know."

"I am the Rajah's guest," I said, thinking of nothing better.

"The Rajah? What? . . . Ah, yes, of course." He seemed very puzzled. In fact, he seemed so interested that he sat beside me in just as European a fashion as I sat myself and stared at me in a very queer way.

"Would it be impolite if I asked you if you have known the Rajah long? Perhaps you met him in England . . . ?"

I was rather embarrassed. I was not sure of myself, and felt uneasy about telling him the true story. He saw it, too, and helped me out.

"You seem to hesitate," he said. "May I suggest that it might be better to tell me . . . not that it matters. You can trust me perfectly of course, and . . . well, please do."

Terribly Oxonian. Terribly nice. Terribly handsome.

I told him.

First he frowned. Then he laughed as one seldom sees an Eastern laugh.

"Shikapur, eh?" he echoed, still laughing. "Would you mind pointing him out to me in the crowd? You see, I've only just returned from England. I'm a little . . . you know."

I saw the Rajah, towering over everybody else, and being the Green Gallant in person with three pretty young English girls and their chaperon. When I indicated him, my new acquaintance practically roared. He started up, then sat down again, and finally stood to his feet. I must have looked as bewildered as I felt, for he said:

"My dear young lady" (he was perhaps one year older than I, mind you), "yours is the most romantic story I have ever heard in India, except the ones out of cheap novels. I think it only fair to tell you that you have been the victim of a joke."

"Joke?"

"Yes. You see . . . oh, it scarcely matters. But actually, I myself am, not the Rajah, but the Maharajah of Shikapur. And I am very glad you have come."

He bowed low and charmingly.

I was covered with embarrassment.

"But . . ."

"Naturally you want to know all about it. Well, the gigantic devil who decoyed you is . . . my very good friend, Bhurlana."

"But why . . . ?"

"Oh, you don't know Bhurlana. He likes the ladies and he is sensitive about them. I can just see his disappointment when you came without the pearl (my pearl, by the way, and you are very welcome to it) . . . so he went off and pouted. You see, we were at Oxford together, and I know him. Every time I go away on business, he rather lords it. We are true Hindus, but both of us have spent so much of our time away that we have rather the European sense of humor. Not a bad sort of chap. I shall have to talk to him."

And with this he walked off into the crowd.

All these events seemed totally unreal. You may picture, if you will, a very dazed and very embarrassed young woman. Every burst of laughter I heard as I sat there alone waiting for Shikapur to come back ... or hoping he would ... I felt was about me and my disillusion. And I could see no reason why *he* (meaning the false Shikapur) should have done it.

Well, he came back.

In fact, the two of them came back together, and my embarrassment grew.

"We have come to beg your pardon," said the real Maharajah, by the way of opening the subject. "You will find Bhurlana very humble."

He did not look it.

"Dear lady," he said, bowing, "you were the victim of circumstances over which we none of us have control, and I come to ask your kind forgiveness for my part in those circumstances. May I have the pleasure of taking you through Shikapur's elegant palace and into his picturesque gardens?"

Before I could answer, the Maharajah himself answered.

"Not at all. Shikapur himself will have that pleasure." And stepping forward he offered me his arm in a manner so assured that I took it, and we went through the hall into another large room which, in contrast to the reception room, was entirely Hindu in decoration.

Once across the threshold, having left his friend staring and speechless, Shikapur suddenly changed his character.

"Miss Crocker," he said, "there is a certain frankness in your face which inspires confidence. It makes me want to trust you in a way which perhaps I ought not. Will you . . . and I mean this very seriously . . . give me your word as an American gentlewoman that anything I say to you within the next few minutes will never be repeated? And will you please promise not to try to draw any conclusions of your own – and even if you do, never to pass them on?"

Mystery, mystery, mystery!

Adventure, adventure, adventure!

I was in my element. Would I promise? Of course I would. Would I keep a secret? I'd keep a million secrets, even if they involved the total destruction of India and the fall of the British Dominion.

I promised. He led me through divers passages into a garden. He brought me to a lawn of rich and perfectly trimmed turf hidden behind hedgerows. He gestured me to be seated on the grass and sat down beside me.

"You see, I have no choice," he said. "If I pretend that this is merely a joke, you will repeat it as a joke and somebody will learn what they should not. I must tell you frankly and trust you . . ."

He looked sharply at me as he said this, and spoke very coldly and sharply.

"We are not bloody people. We may be idealists, but not *that* sort."

I showed my puzzlement. He came to the point.

"You see, you were mistaken for some one else. Some one

else should have been on the steps of the American Consulate at that moment, and should have smiled. It was all prearranged. Well . . . no matter what the reason . . . you were mistaken for that person, and until you came this evening, we did not realize the mistake."

"Political?" I inquired, now regaining a little of my native aplomb.

He darted a sharp look at me. He had power, that young man.

"Naturally I will not answer any such question," he said. "Let us call the whole incident closed."

"In spite of a woman's curiosity?"

"Because of it . . ."

"Oh . . ."

"And, Miss Crocker, may we now be really friends?"

"Have you a harem?" I countered ironically.

He laughed.

"I'm afraid not," he admitted. "I'm too British, I expect. But Bhurlana has."

He paused a moment. Then:

"And about being friends?"

I was beaten. I was really pleased by this charming young man. It was a page out of a romance that brought in maharajahs and slaves and dark, mysterious things and handsome princes, and I was as happy as a schoolgirl.

Could we be friends? How could we miss it?

Indeed, Shikapur and I did become excellent friends, which we are to this day. He became my key to India and the haunting spirit of her in which I had come there to bathe myself.

From Bombay to Benares to Agra to Amber to Calcutta, he was my guide and my interpreter and my companion.

He explained to me those things that the foreign eye and mind could never understand about the mingled, yet separate races of the Orient, and the mysteries and the symbols. And if I have ever drawn into my life some of that beauty, some of the peace and rest that is India's soul, then I have him to thank for it.

But I wanted adventure and I got it.

You will remember how my friend had mentioned that Bhurlana had a harem. Well, I saw something of that tall, handsome man, for his good friend and I had arrived at a basis of courtship, and one day I taxed him on the subject.

He laughed.

"I suppose I ought to put you in your place for such a suggestion," he said. "But as you are as un-Indian as possible" (I resented that) "you are already forgiven for all the *gaucheries* of that sort you may make."

"Why is that *gauche*? You have one, haven't you?"

"Certainly. But that is not a thing we mention with outsiders."

"But I want to see it."

"Ah? Why?"

"I mean, really see it. Live in it for a few days."

That floored him. He couldn't believe I was serious. And after some discussion he began, I was sure, to think I was completely mad.

Nevertheless I won. He eventually challenged me to spend an entire week in his mysterious assemblage of beauties (such, I supposed, they were) . . . as his guest. He declared that I would ask to be released in a day or two. He insisted that no woman but an Easterner could possibly adapt herself to the life. He even implied that I might be shocked.

Naturally, this sealed the bargain.

Headstrong as usual, I left with him and Shikapur for a settlement outlying Bombay where the harem was. On the way I learned a little about what I was getting into and it was far less glamorous than it had been in the abstract.

The fact is that harems do not exist in India as they do in Turkey or in other purely Mohammedan countries. They are not a national institution, and they are not a large lodging house for the legal wives of the richer men. As a matter of fact, they are rather devoted to the mistresses of the richer nobility, and have no place in organized society at all. Had I realized this, I doubt if I would have been so free to accept Bhurlana's challenge.

But I had "made my bed" . . . and so forth.

We arrived. I shall not name the place, because it enjoyed a certain amount of notoriety, and Bhurlana came in for a great deal of criticism from the British Civil Servants and their wives. Nor am I going into the splendors of an Eastern potentate's harem, for you have all seen your cinemas, and read your romances, and you probably therefore know as much about the subject as I do.

Well, I took my disillusionment fairly well.

I was first introduced – if that be the word – to a gorgeous, fat, and really very beautiful mountain of a woman who was the dominating spirit of the establishment. She had the power that comes of priority, and if the owner himself had grown tired of her charms, or had passed on to other blandishments, it was only contributory to the authority she wielded in her own palace.

But there was real beauty there. I soon learned to distinguish between the confined inmates of this woman-colony and the innumerable little dancers, mostly very young girls, who were employed there for entertainment. I found that many of the former were women of considerable culture, and that many had traveled or had lived in Europe. In fact my English and what I remembered of my French was quite sufficient to get me on a friendly basis with most of them.

But hardly had I been given my sumptuous apartments and my attendants, than I realized how completely in the power of the tall Hindu nobleman I had gotten myself. He was God here. They kissed the ground before him. They prostrated themselves as he passed. He was their religion and their idol. It was slavery and despotism, and it was wonderful.

But . . . you cannot put some forty-odd women into one fairly confined space and expect no tension. And tension there certainly was.

First I made friends with a charming girl called Radipurtha. She had been "sold" into the service of the maharajah (although she called it by a nicer name) by her lordly parents who owed his father a considerable sum of money. Banal story. This little girl took the trouble to warn me and finally to protect me. A warning may not have seemed necessary, but actually it was. If the masks could have been lifted from the faces of Bhurlana's favorites, the whiskers of the feline would have been the first things to appear. I will give an example.

You should know that I was the "guest" of the master, and not a regular inmate of the harem. This did little to inspire popularity for me, especially as I was privileged to sit at the right when he deigned to dine in state in the enormous dome-covered hall in the center of the main palace, while at my right sat the young and handsome Shikapur, even more fascinating in his Oriental costume.

The Mountain Woman, whose name I cannot remember,

never took her eyes off me that first night. I made no effort to cover the blondness of my hair nor to color my skin, and I know that I was far more red than white during that first dinner.

The little dancers noticed me, too. I could feel it rather than see it.

Well, that night things happened. I suppose my attitude towards Panya, my attendant, was a little different from that taken by the other women. She was a charming and trembling little thing, and I tried to be kind to her. It paid, apparently.

I went to bed ... really a matter of considerable ceremony, perfuming and oiling ... and promptly went to sleep from the sheer exhaustion of nerves that the day had brought me. Suddenly I was awakened by a scream. I started up and saw my little Panya writhing on the floor. For an instant paralyzed with fear, I did not understand what it was. Then I could see that she was struggling with a snake about ten feet long and whose flat, triangular head told even me that it was a cobra.

Other women and a fat negro broke into my apartment. There was a moment of mad excitement during which I remained useless in bed. Then the eunuch, with a simple movement which I could never explain to myself, lifted the snake near the head and calmly walked off with him.

Panya had fainted. I had, nearly. But I felt no little shame for myself when I learned that it was a fangless, aged cobra belonging to the Mountain Woman, incapable of harm. Still, it was not a nice visitor, and little Panya, who doubtless should have known better, did not recognize it. She would have risked her life to save mine.

Some of the beautiful ladies had played me a rather terrifying joke.

That practical joke ... with its rather mean twist ... will serve to illustrate for you the jealousy and suspicion which reigned in that colony of women.

I have one story to tell which is really odd. I did not witness it, but it is typical, and ought to be written. Some years before my visit to the place there was a murder. The loveliest girl who ever found her way into that questionable paradise was killed by a jealous inmate in a manner that is worthy of mention.

She was taken gravely ill one day, suffered all the tortures of the damned, and died in exquisite pain and agony, in spite of every effort of Hindu art and British medicine. Bhurlana, really fond of the girl, was beside himself. He had an autopsy performed, and the British army doctor in charge discovered that she died ... not of any strange poisoning, as had been suspected, but of millions of tiny perforations of the stomach and intestinal tract by short hairs. Some of those she-devils had put chopped tiger hair in her food.

I need not tell you that I was very careful about my own food after hearing that story.

Another thing I recall was the strange devotion of the women to snakes. I had later in life a chance to observe this from a more personal point of view, but it was first brought to my attention here.

Snakes, when they are big enough, are fascinating even to a woman of my Western culture, but to the Oriental they assume an importance and significance we can hardly conceive. And there is a certain sexual side of the attraction, too, which I am not able to explain but which, I hear, has been recognized by modern psychologists.

There was a sort of feast day. It had a religious meaning,

but its purport missed me altogether, as I never fully understood the many strange rituals of the Hindu doctrine and their symbolic meaning. Part of this ceremony was dancing, and very exotic and exciting it was, too. I sat with Bhurlana and young Shikapur and some of the favorites, while the paid dancing-girls went through their movements.

At the end of the ceremonies, came the famous snake dance which, I understand, was suppressed by Queen Victoria. Personally I fail to see why she should care whether her Indian subjects dance with snakes or not, but I suppose that is none of my business. However, whatever it meant, a naked girl – and not an Indian, either, but a pure negress – appeared with a basket. From it she took a long sleepy python and let him coil on the floor. Then she began a series of movements which were carefully calculated to rouse the sleepy monster to attention. He lifted his head and watched her, fascinated. At the end of the dance, as she reached a point of something like madness, she picked him up in both hands and allowed him to coil himself about her body while she moved in a slow, undulating rhythm.

Closer and closer the coil gripped her. His head peered over hers. He seemed to peer into her face, his tongue darting like a whiplash. Gradually her movements became less and less pronounced until at last she stopped altogether, standing still with her arms outstretched.

It seemed to me that she was growing pale, if that were possible. Then suddenly, before anyone realized what was happening, she toppled over. Guards and women rushed to her. The coils were gripping her with a vise-like grip. She was being stifled. But the extraordinary thing was that she seemed to want to be stifled. She was in a state of ecstasy while her entire body was being crushed. And when they tried to tear the serpent from her, she opened her eyes and screamed to them in protest.

It was a narrow escape.

Well, I won my bet with Bhurlana. But, believe me, for I say it with a certain fervor, all is not beer and skittles in those musty, jealousy-ridden, feline dens. Reconstruct your rosy ideas of them.

But India . . . !

I am going to digress, and give you some of the more fundamental sides of what India became to me. You may already have gathered that there is a strong religious streak in me. I do not mean for one moment that I am a fervent follower of any of the accepted creeds and doctrines. Religion to me has never meant doctrines nor forms nor methods. I believe that the philosophers of today and of yesterday are more or less agreed upon this point also. I have gathered this, not from any study, but from the conversations of those more learned than myself.

There was a reason for my coming to India which had nothing to do with adventure, with the so-called "freedom" of young women who are bored with their lives at home, nor with flirtation (already much too prevalent in this book, I am afraid). This reason cannot be called other than religious. If you want to be hard on me and my insufficient understanding of the mysticism of the East, you will probably say that I was sentimentalizing about what I did not know.

You will remember that, twenty years before the wheel of life had spun and tossed me into Bombay, I had had a vision of a beautiful and radiant woman, dressed in an Oriental costume, lying on my childhood's bed. A glimpse, a cry, and it vanished. But it had remained vivid in my childish imagination, and became in later life symbolic of something that I wanted, wanted to know and to understand.

All through my life I have been drawn to that which I cannot clearly define. The Buddhism of China and its beautiful pageantry fascinated me and became a narcotic to me, as did the rites of the Japanese and their (to me) incomprehensible symbolism.

Thus in India.

Now there are two important influences which threw me into an adventure (a badly chosen word) which colored my entire after life. The first was another vision, and the second was a book.

The vision occurred in my hotel in Bombay, some weeks after my experience in Bhurlana's harem. I had returned from an evening's amusement, and had been dancing, and using those other devices by which we decoy ourselves into thinking that we are having a good time. I returned alone and was tired. My mind was relaxed and concentrated on nothing in particular, and I was so exhausted bodily as to be almost in a state of coma.

I opened the door of my apartment, walked through the ante-room, through the drawing-room where the moon was pouring in like an arc light, and into my bedroom. I went to the mirror without lighting the kerosene lamp which the up-to-date hotel afforded and stared at myself. A very feminine gesture. Perhaps I was trying to convince myself that I was still beautiful though tired.

In the mirror, I saw that something radiant and shining was on my bed. I turned quickly. The same beautiful woman I had seen when I was a little girl was lying there. She was *purdah*, but her veil did not conceal the beauty of her eyes. They were smiling at me. Slowly and gracefully she raised herself and sat up on the bed, drawing her feet under her, and holding out her hand to me. Her clothes were of the richest silks and her head crowned with a diadem of the most glorious pearls.

I was not afraid. I started forward . . . just one step.

She vanished.

Nothing was there. Nothing. I lighted the lamp and saw that the pressure of no body had indented the perfectly smooth bed. But I seemed to be conscious of a faint perfume . . . very faint . . . probably imaginary. That was all.

I could not sleep that night. It was too real, too convincing. But tired as I was, a certain refreshment came over me, and in the morning I found myself possessed of great joy.

Now for the book.

It was a book which had been published a few years before in Bombay . . . the translation of Jogindra's *Hathapardipika*, the book of the Yoga. My friend Shikapur made me a present of it in reply to several rather childish questions I had put to him about Hindu religions. It was perhaps a hard subject for me, but it was, all the same, a great revelation, and it gave me a comprehension of the deeper things of existence.

Yoga is a Sanscrit word meaning concentration. It is today the name of one of the orthodox Hindu systems of belief. It has for its teaching the way in which the human being can become perfectly united with the Supreme Being. There are eight stages of this concentration: self-control, external and internal purity; postures (which have served as basis for many of the false Yoga "rackets" popularized in Europe and America by would-be intellectuals and handsome, money-seeking Hindus); regulation of the breath; restraint of the senses; steadying of the mind; fixing of the mind on the Supreme Being; and profound contemplation.

The Yogin, or follower of the Yogi creed, may attain eight great powers when he arrives at maturity of the *samyama*, the last three of the stages. He may shrink into the diminutive form of the atom or may obtain perfect control and dominion over everything or yet possess a knowledge of all things that have or may happen in the earth or in the heavenly bodies. The Yogin may even attain the powers of comprehension of the most subtle elements and be able to see all objects at once as he approaches the identity with the Supreme and become part of Him.

Perhaps it is not given to Westerners to comprehend or to have sufficient faith to master these conceptions. I failed as all Occidentals have failed, so far as I know, but I brought a great beauty into my life and I can only wish that I were a big enough person . . . I was about to say "soul" . . . to fill my life and mind with the richness of this majestic conception. But to my story.

It begins when, shortly after my odd vision of which I had told nobody, I heard an account of a strange thing. It seems that there was a famous Yogin who dwelt in a cave near Poona and who had arrived at an envious stage of concentration. He practiced what is called the Hatha-Yoga which is the near means to the supreme end of liberation, and he was able, when the spirit moved, to explain any of the mysterious phenomena of life, death, or life after death. Hundreds of soul-hungry persons visited his cave, and some were rewarded, while others to whom he took no notice, were turned away with no more knowledge than before.

An American newspaper man, whom I leave nameless, sailed from San Francisco and paid a visit to Bhojaveda, the Great

Yogin. He went as though on a great Christian pilgrimage of the Middle Ages, on foot, with no guide and no money, in perfect humility, perfect simplicity, and was never again heard of.

There was considerable speculation among the residents of Bombay as to whether he ever reached the Yogin or not, or whether the revelations of the great Contemplation were such that he made an end of his life after the interview. The government attempted to solve the mystery of his disappearance but nothing ever was known, least of all from the Yogin himself.

But an idea was born in me then. It became almost a fetish. I determined to visit the Yogin, if it was my last experience in this life. I finally told my plan to Shikapur, who was seriously upset and concerned, and did everything in his power to dissuade me.

Stubborn as I was, I became even more determined to go. I was troubled by my vision, and by a certain inner disturbance of mind or soul which I associated with it. I was not a very happy girl and I wanted that Great Peace which the *Kaivalya* or true Liberation brings. Call it the sentimental or romantic ignorance of a silly young woman if you will. I was not the first nor yet the last. There was something I wanted. I did not understand but I wanted it fervently.

Result: I went to Poona.

I rode on a mule, accompanied by Shikapur, to the city, through a dark jungle and protected only by a few native bearers and guides and my very worried young friend. Nothing happened, however, that showed cause for his disturbance, and I reached there after five days of slow going, tired, a little frightened, and very sorry that I had come ... but determined to go on.

The cave of Bhojaveda is situated about seven miles from Poona under a low wooded hill. It is less a true cave than a rock-shelter which runs some fifty feet back into a turf-covered gigantic bowlder.

My guide would not approach it nearer than a half mile off, whether from fear or from some religious concept. However, I rode on alone, until three totally naked, blackened men barred my way. I exposed a little note written in Sanscrit which Shikapur had prepared for me. They read it very gravely and slowly and then stared at me. I wanted to cry or to faint. I was afraid to be there and afraid to go away. It was no fear of the ordinary sort, rather a fear of the mystic and of the powers of which I knew nothing. But one man made a motion for me to follow and then walked ahead of me towards the huge cleft of the bowlder.

At a certain distance, the men motioned me to halt and to dismount. I did, and one remained there with me while the other walked very slowly forward and into the cave.

He remained there a long time. Meanwhile the one who had stayed with me stood rigid and erect, his eyes and body turned away from me and towards the cave. A statue.

After an endless while, the first man returned, slowly, with an exaggerated, measured step. He did not look at me. He took his place by his companion and fixed his gaze somewhere, saying . . . in plain English which was fairly understandable:

"Go. It is the moment."

I went forward and into the cave as though in a trance.

Another naked Hindu emerged from somewhere and preceded me down the blackened shaft until we came to a dim room-like opening where the rock had formed a natural internal shelter. It was faintly lighted by a break which ended in daylight far overhead, aided by a feeble oil lamp.

My silent guide stopped and held up his hand.

I stood breathless, waiting.

Then from the shadows there appeared a phantom.

The being who moved silently into my vision was practically transparent. He was a man who was very aged. His perfectly white hair hung to his waist and his beard to his knees. He was without any garment at all and his skin seemed to be wax, and one could notice that the fingers and the flesh of the face were actually translucent. All the veins of his body were as clear as if they had been painted on him.

He stood before me, erect. But I knew that his eyes were not fixed on me, and this gave me the courage to look at them.

They were enormous, lustrous, and seemed to glow, as the light of the lamp struck them, deep in the caverns of his eye-sockets. His face was a skull with transparent wax-skin scarcely concealing the bones. But in some way which I cannot explain he was beautiful. It was an ethereal beauty. There was something of another world in that face from which all color had vanished.

Then, in a soft, clear, sweetly vibrant voice he spoke. It was probably Sanscrit in which he spoke, or some old Indian dialect. He spoke rhythmically and with no inflection of the voice. It was like a machine speaking, like some strange singing or intonations of sounds and accents. And I understood nothing.

But while I stood, too far out of myself for terror or any definite emotion, I became hypnotized by that voice. I was lulled by the timbre, by the rhythmic speech. I felt so far away from everything, and could see nothing definitely.

Then, somewhere in that dim light, I saw a vision ... or perhaps a reality.

It was the image of a young Indian boy, very beautiful indeed. He moved towards me and smiled at me. He lifted his hands half-way towards me. He was dressed in the rich costume of a Hindu noble, and it was remarkable ... I shall always remember it ... that he wore about his neck twelve strings of magnificent pearls. I have never seen their equal for luster.

And then the voice ceased.

And then the boy vanished.

And then Bhojaveda, the Great Yogin, turned without motion, without sound, and silently faded into the shadow.

The naked Hindu was once more beside me. I realized the interview was at an end, and I followed him dazedly back along the passage. I could see the light of the entrance growing larger and larger, but I was not conscious of moving towards it.

Then the sunlight and the air. Then more complete consciousness.

Then I recalled that I had learnt nothing at all, and that I had understood nothing.

The two naked Hindus were still waiting in their rigid, motionless pose. I walked towards them until one of them lifted his hand for me to stop. He spoke to me in English. Years have dimmed my memory of his words, but the substance is this:

"You have heard, but you did not understand. Know that it has been given to you to see what all do not see. The vision you had in your childhood and have again had recently, is a vision of your mother. The young child who visited you in the cave was yourself in your last reincarnation, son of that mother. Once more will you see the vision of the mother who is watching you, one last time, and on that day you will go to her. You have read the Truth, but it is not given to you to understand the Truth. You cannot change what is to come, and you cannot escape it. It is of no purpose that more should be revealed to you."

Now I will make no further comment. You may imagine for yourself the effect that such an interpretation had on me, the more especially as the man who now spoke to me had certainly not been within two hundred feet of the sound of the Yogin's sweet, quietly modulated voice.

I left with a new passion and a new fear. I was inarticulate when I returned to the worried, waiting Shikapur. The East, its depths, its penetration, its mysticism, had gripped me still tighter in its long fingers. My curiosity had grown into passion like a sudden flowering.

But there remained the fear of that beautiful vision which would foretell the end of my life.

But there are other facets to my days in India. A curious story comes from Bombay concerning a friend of mine. I say "friend" with a certain emphasis, because there came a time in Bombay society when I was completely without friends. I had, as you may have gathered, broken the "code," and had appeared publicly with "the natives."

The story concerns a young English girl named Ellen Purling and her stiff chaperon, Mrs. Reginald Benn. This latter would have made a good character from Dickens or Thackeray, but was born too late. I christened her "the Battle-Ax." She was the estranged wife of an M.P., I learnt after three weeks' acquaintance over a dinner table. She had been engaged by the Purling family, who were apparently "good county stock," to escort Dear Ellen on a voyage of education through the British Empire, and at the same time to keep Dear Ellen from the hands of any "impossible foreigner" who might aspire to the well-rounded money-bags of the Essex Purlings.

And this she did.

Mrs. Benn, armed with lorgnette, and a thick fringe of chilling respectability, had routed more than the "impossible foreigners." Even the most presentable and sweet young Englishmen, en route to a good civil service post, had been completely daunted by the weapons of this hardy lady. Much to the harm of her charge, be it said.

Ellen Purling was just 20 when I made her acquaintance in my hotel. She was as pretty, in a sweet-pea way, as a rosy, classical-featured, English virgin can be. I learned after some timid and unconfiding weeks that the only men she had known in her life were her father, the rector of St. Winifred's, Purling, and the rector's son. She became, in time, very friendly with me in spite of the Battle-Ax's first hesitation and obvious *méfiance*. Mrs. Benn rather liked me herself, after the first two weeks. She was a lonely soul, although she did not know it, and her professional ferocity made most people careful not to have any more contact with her than was politely necessary.

Ellen I really liked. Perhaps her diffidence and her innate and starving sweetness contrasted so much with my own hardy and swashbuckling young ladyhood. I was a little envious of her, in a way. I had maybe lost something, in not having that sweetness . . . not being capable of having it. I suspected in her, too, a quiet little unhappiness. It was not long before this was translated into very clear terms.

At all events, Mrs. Benn made a very special exception in my case, and allowed Ellen to go about with me now and then. And one day it happened.

Ellen and I were doing the bazaars and shops. There was a curious little place where birds and strange fish and odd little animals like mongooses were for sale. Ellen had seen somewhere some pet fish that had sunset heads and whose bodies graduated through the whole gamut of colors into one long streaming blue tail-strip and another long crimson one. We were directed to the store in question, and it was really an adventure in itself. But not the least curious and fascinating in the place was the proprietor himself. I have no idea to what caste he belonged, but he had the dignity of a noble, the grace of an Apollo, and the beauty of a god. I can still picture him in his immaculate white turban, his black tunic of mohair, his white and not-so-immaculate trousers and bare feet, his delicate, nervous hands and long finger-nails, and his neatly parted beard which added to his air of a distinguished but impoverished young philosopher.

I was amused at him. But Ellen stared at him with round eyes. I did not recognize the symptoms at first, but afterwards I remembered that stare.

We bought the fish, whatever its name was, and we bought a red, green, and violet bird of some sort and we would have bought perhaps the entire shop if the bearded young man who owned it had not been interrupted by the entry of some chattering young couples in search of souvenirs.

What a way that young proprietor had with him. His limited, but effective English, his bowing, his "Ah, but the *memsabib* would to see be interested . . ." and his really enchanting smile. We went out of his shop at last, complete with aquarium and menagerie. We went to tea – I have forgotten where – and then suddenly I got rather a shock.

"Wasn't he wonderful?" asked little Ellen Purling, breathlessly and radiant as a June bride. "Did you ever see anyone so good-looking? Such eyes? Why, they fairly *compelled* me."

Now I can understand schoolgirl enthusiasm, but I never expected to hear little Miss Prim talking about a man's eyes *compelling* her. She babbled and chattered about him for over an hour, and I was just as astonished to learn that she had found out his name during the first few minutes I had wandered away from her to look at some of the finny wonders of his place. It was Rabani, or something of that kind.

We returned to the hotel, and Ellen asked me, childishly, not to mention to the Battle-Ax that she had talked so much about the shop-keeper. I promised, and that was that.

But that night, who should come to my room in a state of nervous hysterics but Mrs. Reginald Benn herself, proclaiming between sniffs of smelling salts and waving of anxious hands, that Little Ellen had vanished, was probably murdered and thrown in the river, or had been sold into white-slavery by "those terrible natives, the horrid beasts."

I doubted it. But I wondered if Little Ellen had not somehow escaped the watchfulness of her chaperon and gone off to see the night-life of the city with one of those nice young men I had seen about and with whom I had even flirted mildly myself in the hotel drawing-room.

I suggested it, but it made matters worse. Evidently white-slavery was bad enough, but running about at night in the wicked city of Bombay with strange young officers or C.S. lads was unspeakably worse. Perhaps because less dramatic and more probable.

To be brief, days went on, and no Ellen. Investigations of every sort were made, and the hotel was turned into a rendezvous for soldiery, police, and officials, for the next fortnight. And then, exactly one month afterwards, came my part in it all.

I was again visiting the Consulate, in order to get some long-delayed mail from America. Returning on foot to my hotel and all alone, I passed through the crowd of mixed races with English trimmings, sunk in a brown study, when suddenly I heard my name called.

"Aimée, Aimée . . ."

It was whispered and barely audible. At first I thought it was my imagination. But then it was repeated again, almost in my ear.

"Aimée, Aimée . . . wait . . . listen . . ."

Right next to me was a Hindu woman in *purdah*, and slightly behind me a tall Parsee, and several coolies also were near me in the street, but not an Anglo-Saxon in sight. Then I became conscious that the voice was coming from the Hindu woman.

"Aimée, it's I . . . Ellen . . ."

I stopped short. Under the band that concealed the lower part of her face I detected a whiteness that no native could match. Ellen Purling!

"Walk along with me and don't say anything," she said. "I must talk to you. I'll show you where we can talk freely."

You can imagine how I was astounded. But I walked along with her and said nothing. Eventually we came to a densely populated district where Europeans seldom, if ever, penetrate, and then on no good mission.

"Here we are," said Ellen, suddenly, and she turned towards a doorway in a very humble and very dirty house in front of which scraggy children, totally naked and totally unwashed, were rolling about and taking shelter from the intense sun under a stretched-out skin. She walked straight in and I followed. There was something that was used for a stairway, very steep and open in the back of each stair like a ladder of flat boards.

Upstairs was a very decent room (compared, I mean, to the rest of the house) and relatively clean. There were two doors and a window that was partly glass and had its broken panes mended with skin.

Ellen tore off her veil, and stood with the merriest face in the world, grinning at me and at my obvious puzzlement.

"Now don't be stuffy and moral and like the Battle-Ax," was the first thing she said. "Oh, I've tried so hard to see you and to talk to you, Aimée. I have caught glimpses of you when I dared to come near the hotel, but I never have been able to talk to you. I knew all the time you were the only white woman I can tell it to. I'm so happy, Aimée . . ."

Disconcerting, all this.

"Well," said I, "what's it all about? I suppose you know that you have the whole government in a state of fever."

She only laughed.

"I know it, and as far as I'm concerned they will have to stay that way. I'm never going to appear again. I'm dead as far as my former life is concerned. Oh, if only you could understand what I've suffered for years. I've been penned up inside, starving, praying for a miracle. Wanting . . . somebody, something."

"And now . . . ?"

"I've got him . . ."

"Him . . . ? Who?" But I knew perfectly well, and she knew that I did.

"Rabani, the wonderful man we saw together in the bird-shop. Oh, Aimée, I can't tell you what he is like . . . wonderful."

Nothing I could say would change her mind. I pointed out that Mrs. Benn, who was well-meaning in her stuffy way, would be disgraced. But no. Little Miss Prim was quite a different girl from the one I had known in the hotel. She was alive, aglow. She was in love. She had suddenly discovered that which had been hidden away from her for years by stuffy people and stuffier conventions. We talked very frankly about "*him*" ... in fact so frankly that I was even a little embarrassed, well-schooled though I was in human relations.

Ellen never returned. She was married to Rabani in a serious Hindu ceremony. She abandoned Christianity and became a believer in the Supreme Being and in the possibility of humans to unite themselves with it. I have a letter from her, not many years old, telling me of her great and continued happiness.

So that story is finished.

Now let me tell a serious and tragic adventure, with myself as spectator. I had started one day for a restful fortnight with some amusing English people ... some of the few whites who did not believe me an adventuress or a woman of evil ... together with Shikapur. We were going to a place between Bombay and Kaiyan, not more than thirty miles from the seaport.

At the railroad station I learned something amusing about Indian mentality that may explain, in an indirect way, the difficulty the English have had in colonizing them, and in making them like it.

At the Bombay station – one of the world's greatest horrors, half Gothic and half Hindu – I saw several hundred natives asleep all over the platform, the green lawn, and every other place where a human creature could possibly lay himself down. It was explained to me that when the low-caste Indians desire to travel, they never think of consulting a time-table, but merely make ready and go to the station. Now trains in India do not run every fifteen minutes, and there are some which do not run more than once in several days. But the natives merely go to the station and wait ... for days, if necessary, sleeping or eating or talking, until the train arrives.

We reached the country place somewhere towards evening and I found myself in a perfect heaven. Date-trees with feathery tops and the sacred fig-trees with their open-air roots were filled with multicolored birds, parakeets, monkeys and all manner of life. Despite the burning sun, it was fresh and vigorous, and the mansion of European design to which I had been invited was situated on an artificial island in the middle of a rectangular artificial pool, banked by hedgerows and flowers. No American millionaire could have built its equal for beauty, for the life about it, the rich jungle green and the gorgeous sky added to the magnificence of the place and made it into a fairy castle.

In the evening I walked out alone.

The vista of my friend's estate lay before me for over one thousand yards and gave into a large, clear field, which, in turn, stretched out towards the heavy forest. There was practically no town, only a few huts and small squat native houses of the agricultural inhabitants. But there was a great peace, a great nearness to that Supreme Being towards whom millions of Indians strive.

I walked out of the geometrical estate and into nature. Dusk was falling, softly, like a cloud of gray feathers through which the sun poured crimson and cobalt rays.

At one side of the open field there was a house which seemed to be quite modern and Western in design. Attracted, I made towards it across the tall grass of the field, as though I were swimming in nature's green. I was elated, ecstatic.

Then suddenly I heard a rustling in the grass behind me and a magnificent black greyhound leapt past me like a whirlwind. He checked a few yards beyond me and came back sniffing and rather friendly. As I patted his head, I heard a woman's voice calling in English:

"Here Crom, here Crom . . ."

I turned and saw a young woman in cork helmet and puttees coming towards me, running, red-faced and out of breath. She was English, I guessed, and very soon confirmed it. I reached for the dog's collar as he stood to be patted and held him for her.

"Thanks awfully," she said, coming up. "He runs rather wild and keeps me out of breath trying to catch him. You're rather a terror, Cromwell."

I asked her if she lived across the field in the house I had noticed, and was surprised to see that her face became very serious in a flash. She admitted that she lived there, and we talked for a brief moment while she smoked a cigarette. Suddenly she excused herself . . . hastily, I thought, and as though she were not wanting to be seen with me. But that she said she would be glad to see me there again, I would have thought she did not care to know me.

I followed her through the dusk to the house. There was no light visible in it. In fact it seemed to be closed. Everything seemed a little bit odd.

Returning to my friends, I asked about the house and was told that nobody lived there at all.

Another mystery.

Well, I saw the young woman again. We had quite a talk on the second day and we became friendly. She never vouchsafed her name although I gave her mine readily enough, and when I walked right near her house with her, she stopped suddenly and said:

"I'd better leave you here. You won't mind, will you? It wouldn't be understood if you came over with me. But please see me often."

I thought there was something wistful about her, and I was able, at the shorter distance, to see quite clearly that the house was boarded up and that there was no sign of life apparent within it.

Stranger and more strange.

Then one day towards the end of my stay, the young woman asked me if I would care to come and meet her friend. I was a little surprised that she had never mentioned a friend before, and I concluded that this was some sort of a clandestine love affair where the man in question could not marry and could not live publicly with her because of the "Honor of a gentleman" and that sort of rot.

Naturally I accepted the invitation. It was for dinner on the following evening. I made my way afoot as usual across the field and came to the door of what was now plainly a house of the Devonshire cottage type. The shutters were on all the windows, but I could see a faint light within and I had scarcely touched the bell when a tall, gaunt butler in livery admitted me with mournful correctitude.

I was shown into a delightful and beautifully appointed drawing-room, where the young woman received me.

She was radiant. She was dressed in a low-necked dinner-gown of white satin with tufted sleeves and the bodice effect of the time that might seem a little ridiculous today but then had a sweet character of its own. She was really very handsome, in a strong, ruddy, athletic and Nordic way, with her blond hair pulled tightly back and her blue eyes wide and smiling.

"I'm so glad. Mrs. Llewellyn will join us in a moment. Do you take cocktails? Or are you shy of these new fads?"

I took one, served beautifully by the mournful butler. We chatted for a while until a footstep on the threshold and the swish of a portiere interrupted us.

Then I saw a vision.

It was a woman of some forty years, whose hair was pure white and seemed like a powdered wig of the Queen Anne period, and she had the most perfectly chiseled features I have ever seen.

"Miss Crocker?" she enquired, with a soft stateliness and in the moderate, firm voice inbred in the true gentlewoman. "I am so glad you were able to come. Joan has spoken of you often. You will excuse my quiet natural curiosity."

Did I detect a certain bitterness? A hardness? Later I wondered about those first words she used.

"Joan, dear, would you be sweet enough to find my fan?"

The younger woman fairly leapt for it, vanished, appeared, and sat down again.

Conversation wiled away the dinner. Mrs. Llewellyn (not her name, and I knew it) was cultured in the extreme, and Joan (whatever her name happened to have been I do not know for I never learned) was vivid and keen. It was an enjoyable evening.

I left at ten-thirty, and Mrs. Llewellyn insisted that a servant accompany me to my home, although I protested.

"You'll come often, now, won't you? Joan will let you know.

You see, for reasons of . . . health . . . I never appear. Joan is so robust and vigorous. She takes the exercise for both of us."

Again, was she ironical?

The servant followed me to the very door of the small house which flanked the big mansion which had been assigned to me for privacy's sake, and scraped the ground, Indian-fashion, as he left. He was a huge Parsee, and very impressive in his *Sadaro* and *kusti*.

I spoke of the people to my friends the next day, but they had no ideas. They were determined that somebody of no particular interest . . . to them, at least . . . had taken over an otherwise empty house for the summer and they looked upon them as "intruders."

But I never saw either of the women again.

For three successive nights I wandered about, hoping to see Joan and her dog, Cromwell. Not a sign. I was curious, but naturally not very disturbed. On the evening of the fourth day, I went to bed early and did not bother looking for my friend. It must have been towards midnight when I was suddenly awakened by somebody touching my arm.

"Memsahib . . . memsahib . . ." a voice was saying.

It was the Parsee servant. He was excited.

"It would be kind if the Memsahib come now, at once. There is trouble . . ."

It was his look rather than his words that startled me. That usually impassive face was holding back more than it could bear. I sat up, and he withdrew while I pulled some clothes on over my nightdress.

We fairly flew across the sunken gardens, the hedge-bound paths of the estate, into the open fields and across to the house of mystery. The Parsee said nothing. He maintained an obstinate silence in answer to all the breathless questions I flung at him, and I was forced to satisfy my curiosity with my own imagination.

At the door, the mournful butler in his shirtsleeves and liveried vest met us. His hair was a rat's nest from a recent pillow, his face absolutely expressionless save for its habitual gloom. But he showed a certain lack of ceremony.

"I trust you are not too late, Madam," he said, and that was all. He walked ahead of my hurrying footsteps up the stairs.

At the door he stopped and listened. I nearly fainted from excitement and curiosity. There was no sound within. He tried the door. It would not open. Other servants, whose presence in the house I had not even suspected, crowded round. The butler drew himself up with real dignity, and, by a single, crushing look, dismissed them all. That man was a power.

"It would perhaps be wise to break open the door, Madam, but I preferred not to assume that responsibility myself. Does Madam suggest . . ."

I certainly did suggest that he do it. I have no idea why, for I had absolutely no suspicion of what had happened in that room, or what I was about to see.

By nature no man of violence, the butler. First he produced several keys, chose one carefully, tried to fit it to the door. It fitted, but another key was in the lock on the inside. He turned to me, and as though pained to utilize force, said:

"With your permission, Madam," and proceeded to hurl his very large body against the door with unsuspected strength. It was a good solid door, too, and although I thought the house would go down in the crash, it did not yield. He shouldered it again, and this time the lock snapped and the door burst open.

I can promise you that never in my life have I had such a shock as awaited me within that room. A lamp was burning and gave its flickering luminosity to an interior of perfect beauty, perfect femininity and perfect strangeness. The room and everything in it was blue. Blue ... I mean every detail, every single object, the walls, the curtains, the little things on the dressing stand ... everything was blue, from the deep marine of the lacquered flooring, its rugs, to the pale hues of the bed linen, the rich ultramarine of the velvet curtains that shut out day or night, and the delicate blue of the enameled furniture.

But on the bed, shockingly and indecently white against all this blue, and looking even more ghastly than the death they symbolized, were the naked bodies of Mrs. Llewellyn and my young athletic friend Joan, tangled, still writhing in death, they seemed, the hands of the older woman still gripping the throat of the young girl, her face still contracted, her muscles still straining, her head caught under the clasping arm of Joan, their bodies woven together. Not a motion. They were as dead as dead. Their beauty had fled before expressions of agony and the struggle that appeared to have taken place.

The butler kept muttering, "My God, my God . . ."

He remained motionless. He stared at those lovely bodies, still rhythmic, still perfect. The white hair of Mrs. Llewellyn, rich as a girl's, fell over her immaculate breasts and was in turn covered by the curls of silk that were Joan's, almost like stains of blood they seemed so red. And the blue light, the blue atmosphere over this tableau created an impression I have never in my whole life been able to forget.

"What does it mean?" I whispered at last to the butler.

He looked at me blankly and shook his head.

I pressed him for an explanation.

"It would be better for you to return, Madam, and may I ... er ... suggest that it will not be necessary to mention these circumstances to anyone," was all he said. "I will do what is right, you may be sure."

I nodded. I was incapable of coherent thought. I turned toward the door, and there I saw the Parsee servant standing like a pillar of stone, expressionless, fixed, staring ... not at the sight on the bed ... but at the butler.

As I turned he bowed low.

"If the Memsahib will return ..."

"Oh, yes, Madam, he will accompany you," said the butler in back of me. I thought his voice sounded slightly strained.

I followed the Parsee down the stairs, out the door, across the fields. Always in silence. He remained just behind me, never making a sound. In a way, he frightened me. He knew something. There was something between him and the butler. He was anxious to get me out of the house. So was the butler. But there was something between them and I could feel it, and it wasn't something friendly or pleasant.

I began to wonder if what I had seen was all it appeared. I began to wonder why two women ... obviously women of culture and obviously fond of each other ... should have killed each other in such a ghastly manner. I began to recall all the detective stories I had read and to wonder if it were possible that two persons should strangle one another. I began to wonder if this was not staged for me. By whom? Why? I began, in fact, to agitate myself considerably. Hysterics, perhaps. I do not know. I began to fear the Parsee, to wish that he would walk a little in front of me instead of a little behind me.

But that was absurd. Nothing happened. He took me to my quarters and left with his scraping bow. All he said was:

"It is perhaps better that the Memsahib does not remember these things."

That reminded me of the butler's caution.

I returned to my bed. It was already early morning, and the sun was fresh and bright, and I was so exhausted nervously that sleep was impossible. But when I finally arose, a little before tiffin, the vision of what I had witnessed early in the morning was so clear, and the fears and misgivings I had made for myself so strong, that I came to a real decision.

Now I have none of the good, honest, Anglo-Saxon feeling of duty towards society. I care very little indeed about society and I find myself under no sort of obligation to that imaginary force. Under most conditions, I would have kept as silent as possible concerning what I had seen and my suspicions, but in this case my womanhood triumphed where my social conscience would have failed. I liked Joan and was sure I would have liked the remarkable woman who styled herself Mrs. Llewellyn. I reasoned about the matter in this way:

Here are two cultured women, of English origin, living together, hidden away in India. The situation looks a little shady, and suggests that they were intent on avoiding the public eye. The term Lesbian was not current then, but everyone who knew anything about life knew all about that. Then here they are found dead under conditions which seem both impossible and unnatural. Could two women kill each other by mutual strangulation? I doubted it. Had there been a different crime from the one I had been made to see?

These things tormented my brain until finally I decided then on the chance of a double murder by the butler or the Parsee, or both together, or any of the other servants, I ought to tell somebody what I knew.

I did so.

I told Shikapur. He laughed and said I was romantic and that I was either trying to impress him with a detective story, or else that I had had a nightmare. I tried in vain to convince him. At last I made him promise to go with me as far as the field and see the house, and then go and investigate for himself if he dared.

The next day he dared.

I waited for him where I would not be seen from the windows in case any of the servants were watching. He was not gone more than five minutes. When he returned, he was laughing.

"Well you nearly won. It was a good story, but I won't let you tease the others with it."

"What do you mean?"

Shikapur looked at me sharply. He told me then that the house was closed and that he had forced his way in through a back window, and that there was nothing in the house at all, not a stick of furniture, not the slightest signs of habitation, nothing.

And if you think that I was able to convince him that not more than 28 hours previously I had really been inside that house and seen what I had seen, then you are mistaken. I went myself to the house and confirmed his report. In the blue room, which still was blue, there was nothing but the walls and the lacquered flooring. Nothing else. Nothing else at all.

And although I knew perfectly well that things had been moved out in the night, and that every trace of life had been removed by some means ... all except the vague odor of perfume that had belonged to Mrs. Llewellyn ... I had nothing more to say. And I was teased, of course. Of that you can be sure.

I received by mail, several times forwarded to different addresses, a clipping from a London paper, with photographs, saying that the bodies of Lady Maud M.... and Miss Joan P...., prominent society women, had been returned to England for burial from India, where they had died of fever while on an expedition into the interior of one of the lesser-known states.

There was no letter, no signature. Nothing but the clipping.

CHAPTER XXII

Calcutta.

I n recounting that incident, another tragic story has been brought vividly back into my memory.

It happened in Benares, that extraordinary city on the river Ganges. I had taken a small house there, just room enough for myself and a few servants. I lazed and did nothing. I had no adventures, practically no friends there, yet I was very happy and peaceful and gave myself up to meditation and thought and the rich, sober, powerful doctrines that are the soul of India.

One day I returned from a walk to find, squatting cross-legged in the hall-way, a young man engaged in mending the straw mats of rented houses. He looked up at me as I came in and looked through me. I have often been touched by strong emotion in the presence of human beauty, but I must confess that the exquisite carving of the features of that youth ... he could scarcely have been more than 19 ... was as nothing I had ever known in my life. He was naked save for a loin-cloth, and as perfectly made as though carved in brownstone by the hand of some rich-minded sculptor.

If I had known that right then and there some sort of a spark had snapped, if I had realized what the finger of destiny was writing, I might have been hard enough to have reprimanded him for cluttering up the hall and have chased him into the kitchen. That is the way a conventional woman, accustomed to India, would have acted.

But I did not.

As he smiled up at me, boyishly, I smiled at him, and passed on into my room, and promptly forgot him. But I had scarcely changed my clothes and made myself ready for tea when I heard the patter of bare feet behind me, and there was the young man, standing dazed and worshipful. He looked at me as a little dog I had once had used to look . . . as though he simply could not bear any longer not to be spoken to by me and was coming over to put his paw on my knee.

"Memsahib . . ." he said, in a whisper, "Memsahib . . ."

"What is it?" I asked. But he said nothing, could understand nothing, only repeated:

"Memsahib . . . Memsahib . . ."

Then slowly and edgingly he came over to where was seated and put out his hand, very timidly, and touched me on the arm, pulling his hand away again immediately as though he were frightened.

Now it is difficult to tell you what was going on inside me, but it is not a usual experience and there is nothing with which one may compare it. I was pleased as one is pleased when a great dog comes over and manifests a liking for one, but I was a little frightened, too, because there was only one translation of the burning of those enormous eyes . . . love. I have never seen such passion silently expressed in my life. This boy, still in his teens, was entirely consumed with it. He stood there trembling. He was speechless and even gasping. I was frightened a little, pleased a little, flattered, and amused too, and quite touched in the vanity. The latter is what made me do the wrong thing.

I held out my hand to him as one might to a little boy. Entirely unexpectedly, he seized it in both of his and pressed his face to it, making strange groaning sounds that alarmed me. And then, without warning, he sprang at me, unleashed and temporarily mad, like a little wild animal that knows no control.

I had one bad moment. Then I managed to extricate one of my hands and caught him a good, old-fashioned slap across the face. That had the desired effect. He stopped his absurd efforts at once, looked terribly frightened, stared at me for a minute, and then fell to the floor and groveled, muttering something in Hindi by which I knew he was meaning to ask my pardon.

Now according to British law in India, this boy was now a criminal and I could have him flogged and imprisoned. However, I did nothing of the sort. I patted his head, called my maidservant and explained that I was going to engage the young man for a *punkah* boy, and told her to see that he had a bath and some clothes.

She explained this to him, and again he fell down and worshiped me, and had almost to be dragged from the room to his cleansing process.

Well, I was a little ashamed of, and a little pleased with myself. One naturally does not carry on flirtations with children, and still less with Indians of impossibly low caste found by hazard in the service of mending one's mats. But I was touched by the lad's passionate adoration of me. I felt, after some strong self-criticism, that I had probably done a good thing, all the same.

You will be able to judge when you see how it turned out.

The following day brought me a visit from a very large and spongy-looking native woman, a man so completely emaciated that I thought he would evaporate while talking to me, and about six children. My servants would not let them into the house, so that I had to go out to see them, while the servants explained that they were the parents of my new *punkah* boy who had come to thank me for being his benefactress ... Also my servants, who were of another caste, were indignant that I should have had anything to do with the boy or his family and they showed plainly that I had lost caste in their eyes.

The family gratitude scene was pathetic. I understood not one word they said but I gathered that the pittance I offered to pay Mouki (so I discovered he was called) was more money than they had seen in their lives, and that I had become the new goddess of their creed. I had the servants give them something, and I left them scraping and chattering, and that was that.

Well, things went on with Mouki not only being the best *punkah* boy that I had ever seen but following me around like a little poodle and mooning at me from his beautiful eyes whenever I was not looking directly at him. Furthermore, it was marked by some of my women friends who occasionally dropped in, and I am afraid that my arrangement was not quite understood. However, nobody ever does understand.

One day Mouki was taken sick. I did not know what was the matter with him, but he was very definitely ill, and I was heartily afraid that it might be the pest. I had him taken to an American doctor, and learned that the poor boy was dying of typhoid. Apparently nothing could be done for he had stoically gone on suffering and concealing it until his state was so bad that he was really beyond help.

Well, as you may imagine, I had grown very attached to the young man by this time. It was natural, for even if it had not fascinated me merely to look at him, he had rather upset my household, brought his family into my life, and had followed me about like a young watchdog with such loving care that I was often embarrassed. I sent him to a good hospital, had everything done for him, but it was no use. He died in a fortnight, calling weakly after me, saying Good-by, and being sad only that he knew he was going to leave me.

This is morbid, I suppose, and what I am about to add is even more so. But it is worth writing down, if only for the ceremony that attended the funeral.

Mouki was of a caste that cremates its dead. I cannot possibly make clear to you the great differences between the various religious beliefs of India, but it is significant that some bury, others leave for vultures to destroy and consume, and still others burn their dead.

In Mouki's case the mother and entire family took the body from my house, carrying my poor *punkah* boy on a rough litter, and I followed them, trudgingly. Far out of the city they carried it until, on one of the ghats of the Ganges, they came to that place reserved for the cremation of the dead, and there they laid him on a pyre while the flames destroyed the beauty of his earthly remains.

It was very tragic. It was tragedy particularly for the family, and I felt in some curious and twisted fashion that I had been guilty of something which I could never repair . . . It was almost as though I had been responsible for Mouki's death. Absurd and impossible, but that is the way I felt . . . I was glad to be able to subsidize the family with a few rupees. I never missed them, but there was joy mingled with the new sorrow of those poor people when they were able to have enough rice for a while.

The gloomy part of this, the burning of Mouki at the ghats, recalls another experience which is not pleasant at all. The Parsees, as is pretty well known, neither bury nor burn their dead. They take the bodies to what are known as the Towers of Silence, and there the carrion birds destroy them.

Such towers are in Bombay on what is called Malabar Hill. I followed a funeral procession up that hill one day, irresistibly drawn and horribly fascinated. All were in white, all were droning some funeral chant. There was real sorrow there, such as we only counterfeit in our splendid European funeral rites. The body of the lost relative was carried to a raised platform on the hill's top, and then, from the near-by trees, swarms, hundreds of vultures, circled the place and flopped down on those remains to gorge themselves in a diabolical feast, a banquet such as Poe or Baudelaire would have hesitated to describe.

I came away sick.

And as I reeled towards my hotel, down the side of that hill of horror, the dark shadow of a huge vulture flapped over me, high in the air. Something fell from his talons, some morsel of human flesh. I ran down that hill as though pursued by the devil, and never emerged from my room for the whole rest of the day.

But there are more joyous things to tell about India. One concerns another Hindu prince who was quite a different sort of person from Bhurlana and the Maharajah of Shikapur.

It all happened because of some friends of mine. They insisted that I join them at a dinner party which was supposed to be something of a rarity, because our host, the Rajah of K., was an eccentric who gave the most splendid parties.

It took place in Calcutta, where I had gone to visit these

friends. The Rajah lived in a palace that rivals anything you have ever seen in the movies for splendor, and the banquet he offered us was equal to the expectations of the most exigent. But there was one false note. I noticed that our host was under the influence of something. I first thought that he was slightly drunk, but then I discovered that it was some kind of narcotic. I mentioned it to my friends, and learned that, among his other eccentricities, the prince was an addict of the *bangba*, a preparation derived from hasheesh, and that it caused him to be *most* unusual and exciting.

It was, as you may suspect, a woman who gave me this reply.

As the evening wore on, the Rajah paid a certain amount of attention to me. I was not in the least annoyed, either, for he was a handsome man and an entertaining conversationalist. But when he made me a great protestation of eternal love as we walked together about the gardens of his palace, I felt that I had heard all this before and was not impressed.

In fact, when he became a little demonstrative I suggested we go inside.

We did. I did not notice exactly how we went in, nor by what door, but I suddenly found myself in a small, windowless room, with no light except that coming from a small oil lamp. The Rajah faced me with a look in his eye that could only mean one thing. He told me plainly what he wanted. I told him I was not interested, and that I had known schoolboys whose technique was far better. He tried being brutal. He practically tore the clothes from my body while I screamed and screamed. He laughed at me, and said:

"Madam, you will learn as others have that I get what I want. There is no use screaming. No sound can get out of this room."

Things looked bad. He had worked himself into a frenzy, and I was frightened. He threw himself on me, striking and tearing at me, while I tried to evade him round the room. He caught me and held my arms with his powerful hands while I kicked and bit and he laughed in a wild, mad way. He held my neck under his arm, and I thought my time had come when suddenly he made a choking sound and fell on the floor and lay there moaning. I brought over the lamp to see what had happened, and saw that the veins of his forehead were standing out in bunches and that his face was red and congested.

Then suddenly he stiffened, and relaxed.

He was dead, and I knew it. He had been taken with a stroke of apoplexy.

CHAPTER XXIII

The Taj Mahal in Agra, India, *c.* early 1900s.

Oh, India! Perhaps the years that I spent in that never-to-be-understood land were the best of my life. I have told stories of it here, and stories of people, but I never can tell the poetry, the rich beauty of it. It was the last strand of truly free adventure and romance in my life. I returned once more to America and Europe, never to go back there, never to follow that curious call, that strangely beckoning and invisible finger. I have often regretted it, but I was never to return. Even now when I am too old for wandering I have sometimes considered going back there to spend the rest of my life, but I know that the golden memories I have of it would be spoiled, and even the less pleasant ones would have been molded into such realities that I would merely suffer disappointment.

It was the people I loved. The Parsee girls with the white band over their heads, the beggars in the streets, rocking from side to side and crying "Dhurrum ... dhurrum ..." the piper with his *Bansula*, the worshipers before the images of Rama with their palms pressed tightly together. There is a realness about it, a closeness to the origin of things, which we miss in the West.

I have not mentioned the lace-like beauty of the Taj Mahal. I have not told you of Amber, the dead city, inhabited only by monkeys and the ghosts of past glory, nor have I dwelt upon the circles of listeners gathered at the ghats of the sacred river while a learned native recited legends or poems or something that had been fascinating those people for centuries. I have not ... but there is so much description that I have not given. These are simple recollections, and no travelogue. And my memory has grown faulty.

But let me say that in spite of the suffering, real and imagined, that pinches India, in spite of the smugness of foreign rule there, in spite of the impossible bad taste of the new buildings, the Victorian glass furniture in the ancient palaces, the hiatuses and incongruities that have been India since Europeans came there to teach that beautiful civilization how to live like our rather cheap one, India is and always will be a kind of Eden. I could find it in my heart to urge that every girl be sent, not to Europe for that veneer called "finishing," but to India to have an understanding of the meaning of life poured into her and distilled in the sunshine of that agonizing, pulsating, suffering, beautiful country.

CHAPTER XXIV

Aimée Crocker with snake.

Before this book comes to its close, and I am nearing the end now, there is another side of my life which I want to write and which had little in common with the exotic and a great deal with the realistic, and is perhaps the vanity of a woman who has grown too old to play.

You have seen that there were two great influences in my life, men and my passion for the East. I have said very little of women except when they made a "good story." But I have always been fascinated by women, perhaps because I understand them less than I do men. In a sense, I have always been a little afraid of them. Perhaps it is a natural mistrust. But with my wanderings more or less at an end, back in conventional America, I began to live more or less like anybody else and to have the same sort of relationships and contacts that any other woman might have. It was not easy for me. The free life of wandering had gotten into my blood and the result was that my assimilation into Western living was a fairly complicated process.

The American newspapers were not the last to take advantage of this fact. Mrs. Grundy and her clique were given a great deal to think about, and the reporters on the Sunday scandal sheets often made me into what they thought was good copy.

An illustration of this was my experience with Kaa. It also illustrates one of the reasons why women have always been mysterious to me, and it makes a good story for those who never happened to read the papers in those days. They made me out to be a rather scandalous sort of person, but I think the fun was worth it and that the joke was on them. Kaa, I may as well begin by telling you, was a snake. Kaa was a boa-constrictor over four yards long, eight inches thick, and the property of the Princess Mara Davi, a Hindu woman, and a person I came to love and respect as I have seldom done any other of my own sex.

The past life of Mara Davi I know very little about, and it is not very important to my story. When I knew her, she lived in a rooming house in New York in rather impoverished circumstances. I met her at a cocktail party, liked her, talked India with her, and we became good friends in a very short time.

When I visited her for the first time, I was surprised, not to say alarmed, to find, curled up on her bed and eyeing me coldly, a huge, beautifully marked boa-constrictor. She assured me that he was perfectly harmless, and, since he never moved, I soon forgot him as we talked.

We had chatted on for over two hours, smoking and having tea, when suddenly I felt a slight pressure on my shoulder, and turning my head I looked into the tiny, bright and round eyes of the snake. He had slid out of his first two or three coils silently and held his head erect like an "S" over my shoulder.

I was frightened, but Mara only laughed.

"It's all right," she said. "He likes you. It's rather unusual. Don't do anything. Just pretend he is not there. He wants to be friendly, that's all."

Well, I had had no experience with snakes nor could I say that it was to my liking, but I held my ground and continued to talk, although rather uneasily. The snake did not move from its place at my shoulder for at least half an hour. Then I suddenly felt him ooze round my body, and his smallish hard cold head came into my lap. Again Mara cautioned me not to pay any attention to him, but she seemed surprised that he was making such a demonstration.

I asked her how it was that she had such a pet, and she told me that he was better than a watchdog, and that she really was as fond of Kaa as one could be of a fine dog. She started to tell me a third reason, but stopped a little embarrassed, and changed the subject.

I pressed her, and at last she said:

"Well, I keep him also for a bed-fellow. But I supposed you would not know about that."

"About what?"

And then I learned an extraordinary thing. It seems that Mara never went to bed but that Kaa wrapped himself around her body, very gently, and she spent the entire night in his embrace. I was skeptical, but eventually I learned better.

I became intimate friends with the Princess Davi, and eventually I brought her to my own home to live, for I had a very large house and plenty of room. With her, too, came Kaa, and it was not long before I was as fond of him as she was.

One night I had an adventure.

I had retired early, for me, and had turned out the light to sleep, when I became conscious of a pressure on the bed. At first I was frightened, when I snapped the light on, for there was Kaa's head and about a yard of his body on the foot of my bed.

But he came on towards me so gently and slowly that I kept my self-control. On he came, foot after foot of him. When he reached me he encircled me, and his head went under the bedclothes. I could feel him, cold and stone-like, crawling down, and I could feel the weight of his 60 pounds of muscle moving over the bed.

Suddenly all fear left. I was curious. Kaa stopped exploring and came up again. He rubbed close to my body. He gave me a strange, tickling sensation that was, I confess, very enjoyable. Slowly his head moved around my body, slowly, inch by inch, he coiled about me. If I had wanted to now, I could not have moved out of his embrace. He was cool. I could feel the vast power of him. I have never felt so helpless nor so overpowered in my life, and yet there was almost no pressure, no force that one could feel. In a few minutes he was completely coiled about me, his head resting over my shoulder. And ... astonishing as it may seem, I was not afraid. It was like being in the strong embrace of a man. I was more than comfortable.

Then there was a knock on my door. I looked up, and there through the open portal I saw Mara Davi in her dressing-robe, smiling at me. She said:

"He slipped out and I missed him. So I naturally came here. I knew he liked you. Are you afraid?"

I admitted I was not, but was rather glad when she said something to him in Hindi and he began slowly to slip out of his coils and ooze away from my body. She spoke again, and he slowly curled up at the foot of the bed. We talked again for some time, and Mara Davi returned to her room, leaving the snake behind with me.

"He's comfortable," she said, "and he won't do you any harm. Better leave him there."

So I spent the night with a snake.

But that is not all the story. I slept until fairly late next morning. Kaa had not moved. His eyes were open and his head was pointed, but otherwise he was motionless. I dressed, and he watched me. When my maid came in with breakfast, she nearly fainted. I forgot to mention that none of my servants would go near Mara's room until she had locked the snake in his big basket.

Before I went downstairs, I thought I would do what I had seen Princess Davi do . . . coil him around me and walk about with him. I lifted his head and heavy coil, and quite as if he were trained by me he slipped around my waist.

In a minute he was all about me, heavily and strongly. I carried his head and about a yard of his fold over my arm and went to Mara's room to return her pet.

When I went in, I found she had a visitor. It was a young girl whom I scarcely knew, but who had been to visit her before. She was very pretty, about 23, and obviously of good American stock. I have forgotten her name.

As I came in, proudly wrapped in Kaa, she stood up almost angrily.

"Oh," she exclaimed, "give him to me."

She came over to me and almost snatched Kaa's head out of my grasp and tried to pull him away. Mara pushed her off, saying sharply:

"Be careful. That is dangerous." Then she spoke to the snake and made a gesture, and he unwound me and slipped over onto her bed, his regular place.

"When did he start liking you?" demanded the girl, almost as though I had done her some sort of harm. I was puzzled and smiled and made some irrelevant answer. But she persisted, and I was slightly annoyed. I remember that I said something sarcastic, and she suddenly snatched her hat and things and stamped out.

"Now see what you've done," said Mara Davi. She was laughing, but there was a look of seriousness in her face, too. I was bewildered, and I was going to ask a lot of questions when the girl suddenly came back again. She was crying.

"Oh, I'm so sorry. I don't know why I acted this way. I was jealous of you ... I can't understand it. Please forgive me. What a little fool I am ..."

And there was a situation explained. Jealous of a snake ... the ridiculousness of it strikes you at first, but the longer I live the less I am surprised at how little we know of the real extent of human emotions and human weaknesses.

Once Mara Davi went away on a visit to some friends, and at my pleading she had left Kaa in my charge. He made himself rather manifest about my house. Some people did not like him at all, and some were fascinated by him. I observed these two types of people, and the contrast gave me an amusing idea. At least, I thought it would be amusing.

I sent out an invitation one day for a birthday dinner in honor of H. H. Kaa, Maharajah of Amber. Of course there was no such title, since Amber is a dead city inhabited only by monkeys and snakes, but the invitations were accepted, for all that. We Americans have a weakness for titles, real or not. I took especial care that a certain type of my acquaintances ... men of a very special sort ... should learn nothing about the truth of the party.

So they came, some fifty of them, men and women from

every stratum of New York society. The dinner was very carefully prepared. There was a dais in the center of the table that was left mysteriously empty, and when the guests arrived there was much speculation as to what the thing meant. For me, I waited until everybody was a little impatient before I appeared, and . . . if I do admit it myself . . . my entry was superb.

I had a special cold green evening gown made for the occasion, with a long train, and very décolleté, and I wore long jade earrings and emerald studs in a coronet. I came in with Kaa wrapped around me, trying to be unconcerned, and before anybody realized what it was all about I unwound him and placed him on the table, right in the center of the dais.

Well, you should have seen the effect. The very special gentlemen uttered squeals of dismay, and one . . . who was perhaps a little more special than the others . . . was so frightened that he simply fainted, while still another gave one long shriek and fairly wafted himself through the door to the street, all in one act. You might have thought him a fairy.

It was very much fun, and those that held their ground laughed as much as I did. The dinner was a great success, except that the newspapers picked it up and made the story into that of an orgy, based on some vague idea of snake-worship, that was really impossible and very unkind.

That is the way in which most of the legends about me started. If only I could have lived up to them I would have had quite a time.

CHAPTER XXV

The Statue of Liberty.

But let me talk some more about America and my recollections that do not come from the faraway lands. I do not want to give the impression of writing travel stories but instead to put down the impressions of an aging woman who has spent her entire life looking for Life, seeking something that is always there if we know how to find it, and often finding it. It is, after all, people who are most interesting. I once heard a little modern flapper say: "People have more fun than anybody else." It sounds silly, of course, but that youngster knew, in her ignorant way, what she meant, and it is perfectly true.

So we will look back at a few people.

Perhaps the most curious passage of my whole life was wrapped around an Italian fruit-vendor. Shocking? Wait till you hear the story.

It happened when the United States had just declared War. I was in Europe at the time, and I suddenly found that I was completely without funds because of the embargo on dollars. Literally, I mean. I had not enough cash nor credit in any European bank to pay my simple hotel bill; I, who was supposed to be fairly comfortable financially. My adopted daughter and son were literally going without essential food, and I myself was both frightened and worried. The obvious thing was to go back to America, where I had money and could use it, but the difficulty was getting the fares.

Finally a friend in need telegraphed me that a passage had been reserved for me on an Italian steamer, but that I had to sail from Naples. We got to Naples, all three of us, Heaven knows how or on what money, and there awaited the most extraordinary surprise.

The passage existed all right, but when I went, as usual, to the shipping office and demanded my ticket at the First Class Department, clerks' noses went up into the air and very haughtily indeed they told me that I was mistaken, I had only a steerage passage.

Steerage!

I do not mean "tourist third class" nor any of the infinitely more respectable modern traveling methods, I mean literally steerage, with all its horrors, its immigrants, its smells and its impossible quarters.

But there was nothing else to do ... either that, or stay in Italy and starve.

We sailed.

We concealed our jewels under oldish-looking clothes. Yvonne carried my emeralds, my maidservant carried all my sapphires and I concealed all my beloved pearls in twelve thick and neck-breaking ropes around my own very tired neck under a black shirtwaist and a frill. Yet it was a lark. Of course I could not possibly let the fact out that I was returning steerage. The newspapers would have ruined me and I would have scandalized everybody in America who did not know nor understand the circumstances. There was nothing in the world to do but to make the best of it, and this we tried to do.

I shall never forget my arrival on the steerage deck. Yvonne and my son were carrying rolled-up packages in newspapers and cheap roll-bags. We looked so much like every other person in the same class that we attracted no attention at first and we were roughly shown our berths as though we had been the lowest riff-raff ever exported out of Italy.

But the first night Yvonne had a triumph. She was very pretty and you could not conceal it, even in a third-class disguise, and the Captain made a great fuss over the little girl. It was rather lucky because she, at least, had the best food the ship could offer all the way over.

But my case was different. To everybody on the ship I was just another immigrant-woman. I felt that horrible oppression that comes from barriers ... the fact that I could not cross the third-class limit, that crushing snobbery of ocean steamers. Thank God for a sense of humor.

Well, the strings of destiny started to tangle our first day out. I found, by trying it, that I could never sleep in the cabin that had been given us. It was foul and stifling, and, to a person accustomed to cleanliness and comfort, absolutely nauseating.

I had noticed one of the sailors, who, unlike the others who were rather stupid, busied himself about everything on our deck. I talked to him, and found out that he was an American although born in Italy, and I asked him point-blank if there were no way of getting another stateroom. I promised that as soon as we landed he should be well repaid. For a wonder, he believed me, and said he would try to do something.

Late that afternoon he told me that he had asked the third officer who sometimes did rent out his cabin. This charming and money-conscious gentleman was perfectly willing to sleep in a hammock for the price of $150, if I would sign a paper for that sum. As things stood in those days the price was very high, but I surprised him by signing his ridiculous document at once, and my sailor installed Yvonne and me in a very presentable cabin before dinner.

Dinner brought me down to the steerage again, and as I was climbing down the steep and awkward ladder, one of the leering peasants in dirty velours and a greasy beard thought it amusing to pinch my legs which were exposed on the ladder. The whole crowd thought it fun, too, and roared with laughter, but there was one stoutish Signor who pushed the would-be joker away violently, swore at him in Italian, and greeted me very politely at the bottom of the ladder with his hand to help me off. More laughter. More Italian profanity and yelling from the offended leg-pincher. But finally, when I was about to run away from what looked as though it might at any moment become a case of knifeplay and bloodshed, they suddenly stopped their excited yelling and the offender went away.

My rescuer turned out to be able to speak fairly good English. He escorted me to the mess-hall (I hesitate to call it a dining saloon) and seated himself beside me. He was very nice indeed, and very attentive.

During dinner, I learned his entire life's history and his name in exchange for a very pathetic (and entirely false) account of my own presence on the ship.

Signor Jiacoppo da Rocca, it appeared, was a fruit-vendor. Further, he no longer pushed the well-known banana-stand about the New York streets, but instead had financed several of his compatriots who did push them, sold the bananas, rented them houses, and had generally grown to be quite an important personage in the Italo-American colony.

He had come over ten years ago from Brindisi and had pushed a vegetable cart with the best of them, saving his pennies, eating spaghetti, and acting like the classical Italian emigrant until he was able to become the "capitalist" he now was.

Suddenly I realized that he was telling me all this with a reason. The reason was not so hard to guess. He gestured, he panted, he rolled his eyes, he smote his rather plump breast, he breathed fire (and garlic) very close to my face, and, still panting, asked me to walk about on the few feet of deck that the steerage was allowed.

We promenaded. It was moonlight, although smelling of tar and kerosene. I knew that on the first-class promenade deck I might have felt sentimental . . . with another cavalier. And then Signor da Rocca outdid himself. He placed one large hairy paw on my knee and encircled me with the other large and hairy arm and tried to kiss me. I remember how afraid I was that he would feel my jewels.

Poor dear! I naturally pushed him away with the proper indignation. He could never have understood how I felt, and he was seriously bewildered, not to say hurt and crestfallen. He went away in high dudgeon, muttering dark oaths to his Italian saints.

I was amused at the whole ridiculous situation, but sorry for him, too.

Next day he was waiting for me at luncheon. He was all smiles, all waving hands and politeness. He begged my pardon, then ten thousand pardons, he "maka-da big-a meestak-a." And he was very cheerful and courteous indeed.

Then came the surprise.

That evening, after promising wildly to behave himself, he took me out on the deck once more . . . and then . . . he proposed to me.

The scene was beautiful. A masterpiece. The huge ruby ring he wore that looked more like a brass knuckle than anything else, he took off his hand and pressed into mine, saying that I was the kind of woman he "lik-a." It seems that there had been a Signora da Rocca who had passed away only a year ago, and that his home was bare and empty. It seems also that I was his ideal, a serious woman who did not flirt, who "do no flirt-a, who no lik-a da kees-a," and that I was being given a chance to make his home on Bleecker Street once more cheerful, once more happy, to bring his children into his Italo-American world to carry on the "beeg-a beesness" he was going to make.

I wanted to laugh, and even wanted to cry. He was decent. He was very serious. It was perhaps the most honest proposal of marriage I have ever had. I tried to stall and hold off my decision until we got to New York, but he was very determined. Finally I told him that I could not promise definitely until I had seen my father in Chicago, but that I really wanted to marry him. I begged him to wait. I squeezed his hand. I patted his face. I made him feel very happy. It was pretty unfair, but I could not give him any real reason for refusing.

Well, he took it for granted that everything would be all right. He was proud of his success in the vegetable business and he believed he was a "catch" for me. He was childlike and sweet.

That evening he announced our engagement to the entire steerage company, and we prepared a great celebration party to which the first and second classes were *not* invited. It was fun.

There were three accordions, two mandolins, a guitar, tambourines, and a mad little girl who danced a tarantella until I thought she would faint. All the snobbish people from the upper decks crowded round their rail to listen to the festivities. They wanted to come down and dance, but the officials were in on the game and they refused permission absolutely. Da Rocca bought wine for everybody, good red Chianti, not champagne, and we danced and played all night. And, as far as da Rocca and the rest of the steerage knew, I was to be the next wife of a successful vegetable dealer and live happily in Bleecker Street among garlic and bologna for the rest of my life.

Complications came through Yvonne. Being the favorite of the Captain, she was given certain liberties which nobody else in the steerage shared. She wandered freely all over the ship and got to know everybody aboard. I went up to the first-class deck to find her, one day. I was distinctly not dressed for exhibition purposes, I remember, and there was a square-jawed Boston woman in pince-nez and a tailored suit who stared at me as though I were a thief, called a steward and asked him if he did not know his duty . . . concerning me, naturally.

Well, the steward was a sweet, nice young fellow, who knew perfectly well why I was there. He came over to me and with really sincere apologies said that he would have to ask me to go below to my own deck. I asked him to send Yvonne to me, and retreated, rather disgruntled, but nevertheless amused that I, who had always traveled with an entire apartment in first class, should be sent back to "my proper place," because of the complaining of this prim, stiff nobody. Ah, well . . .

Yvonne did not come directly. I learned that she was having the very devoted attention of a young man slightly her senior, and was "unavoidably detained." When she appeared she was all excited.

"Mother," she said, "there is the nicest boy here from California, and he knows all about you and us."

Poor youngster, she was very pleased, but I was frightened stiff at the thought. Well, the "nicest boy" came down to my deck the next day and asked me straight out if I were really a San Francisco Crocker. There was nothing to do but to tell the truth, and I tried for some time to make him understand that he was to keep the news to himself. He never understood, the dear boy, but he promised. I suppose he thought that I was hiding, or had fallen into some terrible catastrophe. He never would have understood my real fear of the newspapers. Result was that he dropped Yvonne as though unclean, but he never mentioned a word. How unjust and how hard youth is! And how tragic! My daughter never understood, and she was hurt.

Well, New York came at last. I was put off at Ellis Island, like any other low-class immigrant, and I must say that in spite of all the stories I have heard about our crude and unkind ways with the herds of poor, freedom-seeking arrivals on American shores, I was treated with every courtesy, as were all the others.

But now comes the cream of the story. My Italian suitor showed himself to be a man of enterprise. He saw us through Ellis Island, my servant (who passed for a niece and who looked much less like an immigrant than I) and all, and squandered a dollar on a taxicab to take us to a hotel. At the hotel we first went to, they absolutely refused to give me a room. They were very superior indeed. Da Rocca was furious, vociferous and raging, but in vain. We continued in the taxi to another even smaller and less attractive hotel and repeated the same experience.

Well, eventually, we located in an almost unmentionable "joint" . . . I can think of no other name for it . . . and there I had to be very firm with Jiacoppo, for he had some ideas of anticipating the marriage we had planned that were not at all in my scheme of things. I am sorry to recall the next act of this tragicomedy. I engaged a suite, two rooms for myself and the family, and he, after much pressure on my part, went off to his Bleecker Street apartment, promising to come and take me to dinner and to celebrate our "engagement" before I left for Chicago.

Scarcely had he gone when I packed my things again, left the bags that were not filled with real valuables, and took my children and servant and taxied to the Biltmore where I was very well known. At first the clerk was as nose-in-the-air as all the others had been, but finally he recognized me and took us in, a little bewildered, but very nice. I was able to dress myself in respectable clothes, telephone my friends and relatives, and finally get to my bank and fix my financial situation.

I never returned to the hotel where da Rocca had left me, but I did buy him the most beautiful diamond ring I could find . . . I mean "beautiful" in his sense; it looked like a lump of ice and was set in an enormous thick gold band. I sent it to him with a pretty limping sort of letter, and indicated no address. That, I am ashamed to say, was that.

Next I got in touch with the sailor boy who had been so kind to us on the ship and paid him the $150 for the mate and gave him another $200 for himself. I have never seen anybody so bewildered and pleased and happy as he was. I guess that poor old ship, if it is still in existence with any of the same crew, will never get over the legend I must have created in the steerage department.

The last curtain of this drama of my voyage was played down about a week after my arrival. I was invited to the home of some friends, an artist who was particularly celebrated at the moment, and his very charming wife. There were perhaps fifty others there, and a very pleasant afternoon party it became.

Suddenly, some one touched me on the shoulder, exclaiming:

"Well, well, what a small world it is after all. Here we all just arrived in the *Savoy* and I meet you in this huge city . . ."

I turned round. It was the pince-nez lady from Boston who had requested the steward to send me back to my proper place.

I was very cruel. I looked at her, straight through. I never cracked a smile. I never offered her my hand. I merely said:

"But, Madam, you traveled first class and I steerage. I'm afraid I do not know you."

She wilted. I was very pleased with myself.

CHAPTER XXVI

Aimée Crocker with dog.

Oh, the people, the human beings of this world! What a kaleidoscope they make with their changing colors, their twisting shapes, their constantly transmuting characters and variegated souls. More than the handiwork of man, more than our bridges, our steam machines, our radios and our x-rays, more than ever our stealing of the birds' flying skill and the marvelous robots and electric eyes that do wonders of work for us, mankind itself is magnificent. The things and qualities we call weaknesses in some and strength in others, the frailties and the passions and the prides and the fears and deceits and cunning of this creature Man is the most full and most fascinating of all study, of all lore, of all culture.

I am closing this book, already too long. I am coming to the end, not only on the paper you are reading but in my own life, my adventures and experiences. But I want these closing pages to tell about humans. I want them to be a passage in review, a parade of faces and minds and bodies and souls, as I knew them and as I remember them.

I wonder how many thousands have passed through the fingers of my life. I wonder how astonished I myself would be if I could only remember them all. I wonder what legions would parade through this book, each with the banner of its own color, his own virtues and vices, his own mannerisms and tragedies and comic incidents. But I have forgotten so many, I have let them slip through the fissures of this aging mind and grow dim upon the fading retina of my recollection.

Yet the ones I still can see, each with a little spot of light shining over him, each with some special tang or flavor peculiar only to him, incidental to my life, a bright patch in the tapestry of my existence.

And I have been privileged. So many of them have made themselves known to a curious world. So many have attained fame . . . or notoriety. So many of them have been publicized and written about and explained as I could never hope to do. And yet . . . my small recollection, my little, sometimes intimate, sometimes incidental, piece of those human puppets that I stole from them and have hidden away in the hiding places of my brain and heart . . . perhaps it is worth while. At least I like to think so, and I will toss them on to these pages for you to smile or frown at.

Who and how many are alive today who remember New York's most curious figure of the twentieth century, Chuck Connors? Most of us have left this world for the Unknown. There are very few of my day who still cling on to life. But Chuck Connors, splendid and mysterious, a ruffian and a gentleman, a nobleman and an apache, still a legend in New York's saga . . . I could not close this book without waving farewell to his memory.

What shall I tell you about him? That his wife died in my arms? That he silently ruled the Underworld, that he was the Bowery king, the "open sesame" of the hinterland of lower New York where even the police never ventured save in numbers and armed? I can picture him still . . . hard-faced and strong, with the look of a handsome man, powerful in body, a walk in which every step seemed to say, "I go where I choose, unmolested, the master," dark, with those triangular eyes that fighters have.

It has been said of me that I collect people as others collect postage stamps. I used to resent it, but now I think it is probably true. I "collected" Chuck Connors (or did he collect me, I wonder?) and brought him frequently to my house in New York where he became one of the more spectacular members of a very varied assortment. It amused him. I suspect that I amused him, too, and that was fair enough because it was natural. It was through him that I had the privilege of seeing what was behind the scenes of New York, and peering into the dregs of that cauldron.

And let the modern, self-styled sophisticate not pride himself that today we are more enlightened on those "abnormal" facts about existence which are today paraded all too plainly. Let me tell you that Chuck Connors took me into that notorious institution (of which you may never have heard if you are young enough) called Parisis Hall. It was an institution for men only. Trusting you to understand with true modern perception, I shall only add that the gentlemen were such that my presence was not noticed. Perhaps I was fortunate.

Others pass in this parade. Oscar Wilde, who was not busy shocking England in that day, was a frequent visitor at my San Francisco home. I am aware of the gigantic structure of naughtiness which the world has hung around the neck of his memory, but I must say, if my timid and unimportant voice can whisper a defense ... if he needs defending ... that I found Mr. Wilde a charming gentleman, fascinating as much for his courtly manner to women as for the pungency of his wit.

An incident? Yes, I can remember several. Here is one, amusing and quickly told. After a dinner given at my home in San Francisco, the other invited gentlemen decided that it would be an amusing thing to drink Mr. Wilde "under the table." A deep and dark plan was laid. I was a party to it, although not an active one. The idea was that if he should relax his guard in drinking, he might reveal some of the things which had already caused scandal.

The drinking started with champagne after dinner. Oscar Wilde dominated the conversation . . . the only tiresome thing I could detect in him . . . and the glasses clinked. At ten o'clock, there was far more boisterous talk and very much less wit, except for Mr. Wilde who seemed to expand and grow more than ever magnificent in his repartee. At midnight, some of the gentlemen had withdrawn from the contest, and others were decidedly red in the face. At two o'clock, Mr. Wilde threw consternation into the conspiracy by demanding gin instead of whisky, and pouring an enormous glass of it for each of his fellow drinkers as well as for himself.

At three o'clock in the morning, Mr. Wilde came suddenly to the realization that he had been making pretty witticisms to an audience that was snoring soundly and had been out of conversation for twenty minutes. He filled himself another gin, tossed it off neatly, and said to me that really he was quite sleepy and would retire. The would-be tipplers had to be carried to their rooms by my servants, but Wilde never even suspected the plot. He was really magnificent.

Wilde recalls another literary figure, Edgar Saltus.

He was the nearest in perfection to sheer physical beauty I have ever had the privilege of knowing. I do not merely mean sensuously attractive. He was radiant of power and will and dash and excitement and pithy wit and all that women hope to find in the ideal male. I met him ... at a dinner party given by Roosevelt Schuyler. It was as though I walked innocently into a spider's web, and as though the spider were a polished, ironic, master-mind who knew every trick of fascinating women, and who spun around me an invisible web of magic gauze that ensnared me and tangled me up in its very comfortable tissue.

We were off, so to speak.

For three years I lived and thought and had heartbeat only in the sunshine of Edgar Saltus. He glittered beside me in Paris, in London, in Central Europe, my cavalier, my Lancelot, my Don Juan, my Faustus. I could bore you and please myself with a recollection of Lake Como which is an idyll that only Stendhal ... or Saltus ... could make worthy of print. I could ...

But I must go on. They glitter in their parade, they are crowding and pressing to be written down, and my book is at its close.

Caruso, Enrico Caruso, the former blacksmith whose voice was like a rich mine of gold. He too came into my collection and sang often in my home. Once for charity, and on that day Anna Held took up the offering of my guests for those who could not live as we did.

Then there was De Max, the strange Roumanian actor who made stage history, and very nearly made me into a page of it; Gaby Deslys, that charming and slightly devilish little creature whom the play-going world loved and now can weep over; Mrs. Leslie Carter, Belasco, Raymond Hitchcock, Diamond Jim Brady, the Barrymores, John Drew, Lillian Russell ... the whole panorama pour themselves through my mind. I cannot take the space nor impose the time upon you to give you each one his little incident that gives them just their own one bright color in my memory. But these theatrical names bring a homely and amusing story back to me. It concerns my husband, Harry Gillig, and it happened in Malta.

Malta, as you may not know, possesses an opera. It is not great, as operas go, but it was remarkable in that some of the loges were equipped with comfortable beds. Yes, that is what I meant to put: Beds. Well, my husband, who had a sense of humor, and who all his life had adored music and worshiped the opera, had a passionate desire to hear one in bed. We went, a group of three of us. Hardly had the first note of the overture sounded when Harry withdrew to the alcove behind the loge where the bed was, and promptly undressed himself and got in. We had a great deal of fun about it with him, but he insisted that the opera had never been so pleasant nor seemed so artistic as when he lay listening to it in a state of reverie in the curious little bedroom of his loge.

But we were talking of people. Husbands, at best, have little to do with "people." I know, because I have had a certain number of them.

When I look back I am inclined to be envious of the young woman I once was, and rather pleased with having been her. For it seems to me that I was privileged to be alive in the most glorious times since the renaissance ... I mean the closing "Nineties" which you can see so magnificently pictured by understanding souls like Toulouse-Lautrec.

You hear today a great deal of chatter about pre-War Paris, and yet almost invariably from persons who are too young to have known those gallant days of the Boulevardier. Not long ago the newspapers devoted a little space to the death of Boni de Castellane, the very last of those magnificent gentlemen. A little space, a few lines on a type machine, and yet that great boulevardier was the symbol of a whole, extinguished civilization. With him passed the memory of Babette and Palmier's Bar, the heyday of Maxim's, Maurice, the efficiently mysterious and mysteriously efficient Parisian. With him passed the last vestige of those days when the Boulevards had a meaning and a culture, the days when wit was superior to learning, when heaviness was a criminal offense, when every word of conversation was a rapier with which to thrust and parry.

Even the scandals of that day were in better taste. They were amusing. Today they are morbid or vulgar or dull. Where has that wit gone, and why has that lightness of touch been allowed to fade? Does there exist today another gypsy violinist who could run away with a Prince de Chimay? Can one hear La Glu and feel her rich, full, earthy character blossoming in the Montmartre that is dead? Where is Nina-Patte-en-l'air? When did Madame Fromage die? Yvette Guilbert struggles on alone, still a noble, richly talented woman, but an old woman now. Yvonne Georges is dead. Phonograph records try to preserve the madness of her "P'tit Bossu" and the heartiness of her "Chant de Marin."

In New York, Sherry's is forgotten, Reisenweber's is a legend, Rector's a tradition and the Gibson Girl a banality.

But to these things I could add many more, and say that they are still alive to me, and still near-by. I am glad that I have lived.

Well, here we are at the end.

I look back over these pages and think that perhaps I was foolish to have written them. Some people who know me indifferently well, will believe that it is vanity. But no, my vanity died several birthdays ago. And yet I have been trying to find another reason for them besides that love of life which makes me feel that I would wish to live all this over and over and over again. Even the mistakes that I made were worth the making. I would make them again, too.

So suppose we admit that there is no particular reason, and that the fun I have had in going over those dim details is the last fun I am likely to have in this life. For one of these days now, I am going to see the vision of a beautiful Hindu woman on my bed, so the Yogin told me, and I am going away where none of this matters very much.

There is a little poem by Fernand Gregh which very few people know and which ends as I want this book to end:

"... *mais j'aurai bu ma joie au Grand Festin sacré*
Que voudrais-je de plus?
J'aurai vécu
Et je mourrai."

—ᨑ—